RUSSIA

RUSSIA

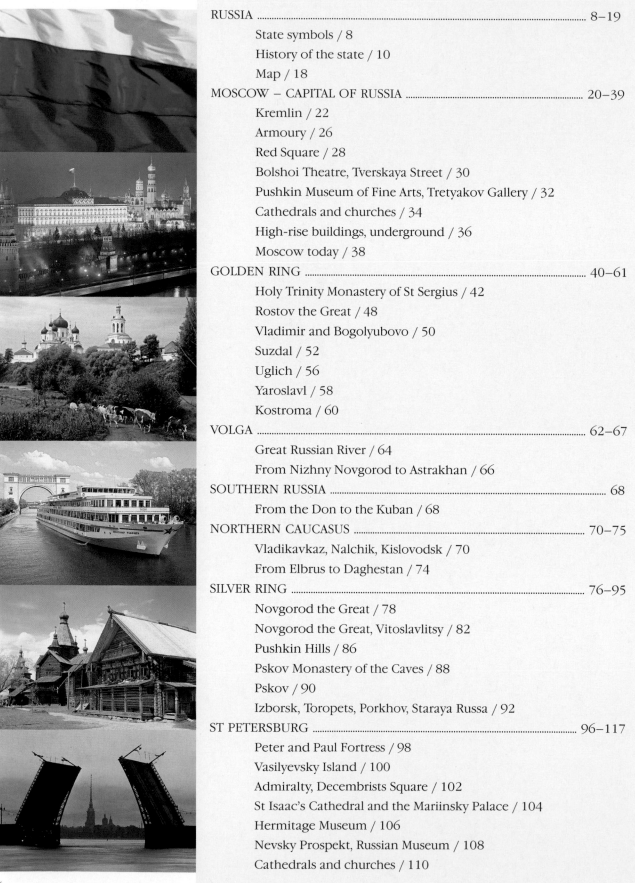

RUSSIA 8–19
    State symbols / 8
    History of the state / 10
    Map / 18
MOSCOW – CAPITAL OF RUSSIA 20–39
    Kremlin / 22
    Armoury / 26
    Red Square / 28
    Bolshoi Theatre, Tverskaya Street / 30
    Pushkin Museum of Fine Arts, Tretyakov Gallery / 32
    Cathedrals and churches / 34
    High-rise buildings, underground / 36
    Moscow today / 38
GOLDEN RING 40–61
    Holy Trinity Monastery of St Sergius / 42
    Rostov the Great / 48
    Vladimir and Bogolyubovo / 50
    Suzdal / 52
    Uglich / 56
    Yaroslavl / 58
    Kostroma / 60
VOLGA 62–67
    Great Russian River / 64
    From Nizhny Novgorod to Astrakhan / 66
SOUTHERN RUSSIA 68
    From the Don to the Kuban / 68
NORTHERN CAUCASUS 70–75
    Vladikavkaz, Nalchik, Kislovodsk / 70
    From Elbrus to Daghestan / 74
SILVER RING 76–95
    Novgorod the Great / 78
    Novgorod the Great, Vitoslavlitsy / 82
    Pushkin Hills / 86
    Pskov Monastery of the Caves / 88
    Pskov / 90
    Izborsk, Toropets, Porkhov, Staraya Russa / 92
ST PETERSBURG 96–117
    Peter and Paul Fortress / 98
    Vasilyevsky Island / 100
    Admiralty, Decembrists Square / 102
    St Isaac's Cathedral and the Mariinsky Palace / 104
    Hermitage Museum / 106
    Nevsky Prospekt, Russian Museum / 108
    Cathedrals and churches / 110

Summer Gardens, rivers and canals / 112

Tsarskoe Selo and Peterhof / 114

BALTIC ENCLAVE OF RUSSIA 118

Kaliningrad / 118

NORTHERN RUSSIA 120–137

Valaam / 122

Solovki Islands / 124

Arkhangelsk, Murmansk, Belomorye / 126

Kizhi / 130

Kargopol, Belozersk, Kirillov / 132

Vologda, Totma, Veliky Ustyug / 134

THE URALS 138–143

Between Europe and Asia / 138

Ekaterinburg, Perm, Chelyabinsk, Ufa, Orenburg / 142

POLAR REGION 144–153

Beyond the 67th Parallel / 146

Taimyr and Yakutia / 148

Peoples of the Far North / 150

SIBERIA 154–165

Taiga and rivers / 154

From Tyumen to Krasnoyarsk / 156

Altai and Sayan Mountains / 158

Baikal and Angara / 162

Buryatia and Tuva / 164

FAR EAST 166–171

Amur, Khabarovsk, Maritime Region / 166

Sakhalin and the Kuril Islands / 168

Kamchatka / 170

LIFE AND TRADITIONS 172–191

The Russian people / 174

National festivals / 176

Bath-houses, ice holes, fist fighting / 178

Fishing / 180

Hunting / 182

Eating customs / 184

Folk art and crafts / 188

RELIGION 192–195

Orthodoxy / 192

Islam, Catholicism, Judaism, Buddhism / 194

COUNTRY AND PEOPLE 196–207

Industry and science / 198

Armed forces / 200

Culture and art / 202

Relaxation and entertainments / 204

The first Russian national anthem was written by composer Prince Alexander Lvov and poet Vasily Zhukovsky. Composed in December 1833, it began with the words God, save the Tsar. *In 1918,* The Internationale *was adopted as the official song of the Russian Soviet Federated Socialist Republic, later becoming the anthem of the Soviet Union. On 1 January 1944, the new Soviet anthem was played for the first time on the radio. The music was written by composer Alexander Alexandrov and the words were written by poets Sergei Mikhalkov and Gabriel El-Registan. The current national anthem uses the same music with a revised text.*

The first official coat of arms was adopted by Grand Prince Ivan III in the late fifteenth century. In May 1857, the national emblem became a double-headed eagle accompanied by symbols of the various territories of the Russian Empire. The Soviet coat of arms was a globe surrounded by wheatears and ribbons inscribed with the words Workers of the World Unite *in the languages of the fifteen national republics. The current coat*

1

2

Russia is the largest country on earth, covering 17,075,000 square kilometres. Occupying the eastern part of Europe and the northern part of Asia, Russia is washed by the Arctic Ocean on the north and the Pacific Ocean on the east. To the west and south-west, the country has exits to the Atlantic Ocean. Russia spreads over eleven time zones. When it is midnight in Moscow, it is ten o'clock in the morning on the islands of the Bering Sea.

The Russian plain extends throughout the western part of the country, as far as the Urals, which run from the Arctic Ocean to the steppes of Kazakhstan. Beyond the Ural Mountains stretches the West Siberian plain. To the east, between the River Lena and River Yenisei, is the Central Siberian Plateau.

3

The Russian plain is bordered on the south by the Caucasian mountain range. The Rivers Ob and Yenisei flow into the Arctic Ocean from the Altai and Sayan Mountains. The Sayan Range is bordered on the east by the mountains of the Baikal region. The Verkhoyansk and Chersky Ranges lie to the east of the Central Siberian Plateau. In the Far East, the Sikhote-Alin Range runs parallel to the shore of the Pacific Ocean. The Kamchatka peninsula is also mountainous.

The State structure of the Russian Federation is defined by the Constitution passed on 12 December 1993. The Head of State of Russia and the Supreme Commander-in-Chief of the armed forces is the President, who is elected for a four-year term by secret ballot based on general egalitarian and direct voting law. The Russian State legislative body is the bicameral Federal Assembly (Council of the Russian Federation and the Russian State Duma). Executive powers are held by the Government of the Russian Federation. The Chairman of the Government is appointed by the President with the agreement of the State Duma. According to official figures on 1 January 2000, Russia is inhabited by 145.9 million people and 130 nationalities. 78.5% of the population lives in the European half of the country. The overwhelming majority of citizens are Russians.

of arms is a shield and golden double-headed eagle with two crowns holding an orb and sceptre.

1. Flag of the Russian Federation
2. Coat of arms of the Russian Federation
3. On the state border
4. The Russian constitution was adopted following a national vote on 12 December 1993
5. The White House is the home of the Russian government
6. The Kremlin
7. President Vladimir Putin

The Eastern Slavs were pagans and worshipped many gods. Dazbog (also known as Jarilo or Hors) was the god of the sun. Stribog was the god of the wind, Perun was the god of thunder and Veles was the god of cattle and wealth. When winter came to an end, the Slavs welcomed spring by baking round pancakes symbolising the sun and burning straw effigies of winter. The Eastern Slavs revered the dead. They buried their princes with great solemnity, building enormous burial mounds above the sites of their cremation and burial. When a prince died, his wife and horses were put

At the start of the first millennium, the European territory of modern Russia was inhabited by East Slavonic tribes. One of the tribal associations was based around the Rhos or Rus tribe on the River Rhos (a tribute of the Dnieper). Later, all Eastern Slavs became known as Ruses and the territory on which they lived was called Rus.

In 862, a member of one of the northwestern Slavonic tribes, Rurik, was invited to come and rule over Novgorod. This paved the way for the first ruling dynasty in Rus. After Rurik's death, his descendants settled in the city of Kiev, which became the centre of Old Russia, otherwise known as Kievan Rus.

In 988, Grand Prince Vladimir of Kiev was baptised. The prince was known as "Vladimir the Fair Sun" for his efforts in uniting and strengthening the Russian State, building new towns and introducing a new faith and culture. The adoption of Christianity as the official state religion had important consequences for the spiritual development of Rus, which now stretched from the River Bug to the Baltic Sea.

In the eleventh century, Rus split up into several princedoms. For many years, the rulers engaged in bloody internecine warfare. In the thirteenth century, the weakened Russian lands were invaded by Tatar-Mongol hordes from the east and Germans and Swedes from the north. The Tatar-Mongol yoke lasted for more than two centuries. Towns and villages were burnt and pillaged; people were killed and enslaved. Yet the invaders were unable to break the spirit of the Russian people. Rus acted as a bulwark, saving the rest of Europe from invasion by the Asiatic hordes.

In the fifteenth century, Rus finally secured its independence. Grand Prince Ivan III made Moscow the capital of a centralised state. During his reign, Moscow increased five times in size. In 1547, Ivan the Terrible was the first ruler to crown himself "tsar of all Rus." He conquered the khanates of Kazan and Astrakhan, assimilated western Siberia and annexed Bashkiria and Kabarda. Eastern Siberia was incorporated into Russia in the seventeenth century.

to death and buried alongside him. A suit of armour, guns, household objects and food and drink were placed in the grave. The funeral was accompanied by a wake and military display. Funerals of common men were more modest. Only the most essential objects were placed in the grave. The Slavonic group of languages forms one of the major components of the great Indo-European language family. It stands on an equal footing with the Roman lan-

Ivan the Terrible's son Fedor was the last member of the Rurikid dynasty. After his death in 1598, famine broke out, leading to waves of unrest. Pretenders to the throne appeared, claiming to be Ivan the Terrible's dead son, Tsarevich Dmitry. False Dmitry I at the head of the Polish forces took advantage of the confusion and entered Russia, capturing and looting Moscow. The country was on the verge of ruin. In 1612, Russian volunteers liberated the capital and expelled the foreign invaders. As the people set about restoring their ruined economy, state and lives, Russia rose again from the ashes. The Land Council met in 1613 to elect a new tsar — Michael Romanov.

guages, the Germanic and also such solitary surviving representatives of ancient groups as Greek.

8. *Calling of the Prince.*
   Artist Alexei Kivshenko
9. *Baptism of Prince Vladimir.*
   Artist Fedor Bronnikov
10. *Trial by Fire.* Artist Ivan Bilibin
11. *Foundation of Moscow.*
    Artist Apollinary Vasnetsov
12. *Battle on the Ice*
13. *Single Combat of Peresvet and Chelubei.* Artist Mikhail Avilov
14. *Yermak Conquering Siberia.*
    Artist Vasily Surikov
15. *Ivan the Terrible and Son Ivan on 16 November 1581.* Artist Ilya Repin
16. *Citizen Kozma Minin and Prince Dmitry Pozharsky.* Artist Mikhail Scotti
17. *Last Minutes of False Dmitry I.*
    Artist Carl von Wenig
18. *Tsar Michael Romanov Sitting with his Boyars in the State Room.*
    Artist Andrei Ryabushkin
19. *Boyarynya Morozova.*
    Artist Vasily Surikov
20. *Morning of the Streltsy Execution.*
    Artist Vasily Surikov

He single-handedly changed the course of Russian history, turning the country into a powerful state ranking alongside the other European powers. He founded the Russian navy, a regular army and heavy industry. A new capital called St Petersburg was built at the mouth of the River Neva, on lands taken from Sweden during the Great Northern War. Peter the Great died in 1725. Throughout the rest of the eighteenth century, the Russian throne was occupied by a series of women, who came to power in palace coups. They continued the work begun by Peter the Great, making Russia one of the most powerful countries in Europe. Following wars with Turkey, Russia gained an exit to the Black Sea. Catherine the Great annexed the Crimea and joined in the partition of Poland, gaining the western Ukraine, White Russia and parts of Lithuania and Courland.

The nineteenth century was a period of glittering achievement in Russian science and literature. The list of great scientists included Nikolai Lobachevsky, Sofia Kovalevskaya, Dmitry Mendeleyev, Alexander Butlerov, Nikolai Pirogov, Pavel Yablochkov, Alexander Popov, Nikolai Zhukovsky, Konstantin Ciolkowski, Vladimir Vernadsky and Ivan Sechenov. This dazzling array of names was accompanied by such Nobel Prize winners as Ivan Pavlov, Ilya Mechnikov and Kliment Timiryazev.

Russian explorers made many important discoveries in the nineteenth century. Fabian von Bellingshausen and Mikhail Lazarev discovered the Antarctic in 1820.

Russia gave world literature the works of Alexander Pushkin, Leo Tolstoy, Fedor Dostoyevsky and Anton Chekhov. Such great composers as Mikhail Glinka, Peter Tchaikovsky, Modest Mussorgsky and Nikolai Rimsky-Korsakov also came from Russia. Russian culture made an important contribution to the development of twentieth-century art. The avant-garde movement paved the way for modernism. Such masters as Wassily Kandinsky and Kazimir Malevich were at the forefront of abstract art. Sergei Diaghilev's Saisons Russes *took European theatres by storm, while the compositions of Sergei Rachmaninov and Alexander Scriabin revolutionised world music.*

21. *Taking of Azov on 18 July 1696.*
    Artist Sir Robert Kerr Porter
22. *Peter I.* Artist Valentin Serov
23. *Empress Elizabeth Petrovna in Tsarskoe Selo.*
    Artist Yevgeny Lanceray

Michael Romanov was succeeded by his son Alexis in the mid-seventeenth century. During his reign, Russia regained the vast territories in the south-west known as the Ukraine, including Kiev.

Russia underwent important transformations under Alexis' son, Peter the Great. The subject of countless books, films and works of art, Peter is probably the most famous member of the Romanov family.

In the nineteenth century, Russia continued to grow in influence and power, leading to clashes with other European nations. In 1812, the country was invaded by Napoleon. Although the French ravaged much of the country and burnt Moscow, Fieldmarshal Mikhail Kutuzov and the Russian army expelled the invaders. Russia absorbed Finland and the northern Caucasus in the first half of the nineteenth century.

24. *Portrait of Empress Catherine II.*
    Artist Dmitry Levitsky
25. *Suvorov Crossing the Alps.*
    Artist Vasily Surikov
26. *Napoleon in the Kremlin.*
    Artist Vasily Vereschagin
27. *Uprising on Senate Square on
    14 December 1825 in St Petersburg.*
    Artist Carl Collmann.
    That day, on Senate Square,
    several regiments refused to swear
    the oath to Nicholas. The tsar
    acted promptly and decisively.
    He surrounded the rebels with
    loyal forces and gave the order
    to open fire on them.
    The December Revolution was
    harshly suppressed. Five of the
    ringleaders were executed, while
    120 active participants were exiled
    or sentenced to hard labour.

In 1853, Turkey declared war on Russia, followed by Great Britain and France. The Russian defeat in the Crimean War demonstrated the need for urgent reforms. In 1861, Tsar Alexander II emancipated the serfs and brought the Caucasian War to an end. He also liberated the Balkans from their Turkish overlords during the wars of 1877—78.

At the start of the twentieth century, Russia was one of the world's top five countries in terms of industrial output. The economic and political crisis following defeat in the Russo-Japanese War, however, led to the 1905 revolution. In 1913, the country celebrated the tercentenary of the House of Romanov. The limitations of the autocratic system of government became apparent

28. *Emancipation of the Serfs
    on 19 February 1861*
29. *Portrait of Alexander Pushkin.*
    Artist Orest Kiprensky
30. *Portrait of Leo Tolstoy.*
    Artist Ivan Kramskoi
31. *Portrait of Fedor Dostoyevsky.*
    Artist Vasily Perov
32. *Portrait of Modest Mussorgsky.*
    Artist Ilya Repin
33. Nicholas II and family. 1905
34. Reconstruction of the murder
    of Grigory Rasputin at the Yussupov
    Palace in St Petersburg
35. Composer Peter Tchaikovsky
36. Writer Anton Chekhov
37. Chemist Dmitry Mendeleyev
38. Artist Ilya Repin
39. In the trenches of the First World War
40. News of the overthrow of the tsar
    reaches the front. 1917

The German army invaded Russia on 22 June 1941, dividing the lives of people into "before" and "after" the war. The Great Patriotic War was the central and most decisive theatre of action during the Second World War. Seventy-seven percent of the German army was thrown against the Soviet Union, including the highest number of tanks and aircraft. The Germans plundered and pillaged, killing and enslaving civilians and bombing towns and villages.

Hungary, Romania, Finland and Italy joined in the attack against the Soviet Union. The Axis powers captured a large part

41

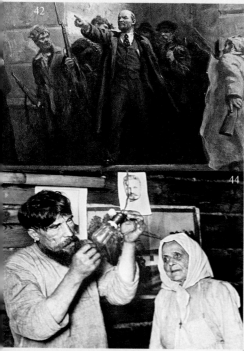

42

44

43

during the First World War. In February 1917, two months after the murder of Grigory Rasputin, Nicholas II was forced to abdicate. Russia entered a new period in its history.

The Bolshevik party seized power in October 1917, establishing a dictatorship of the proletariat and nationalising all property. The Bolsheviks were known as Soviets, as their main slogan was "all power to the Soviets." The new government was headed by Ulyanov (Lenin). Civil war broke out in 1918, lasting four years. After a period of War Communism, the Bolsheviks were obliged to introduce a number of capitalist reforms, known as the New Economic Policy (NEP). The Union of Soviet Socialist Republics was formed in 1922. Joseph Stalin embarked on a policy of rapid industrialisation and the collectivisation of agriculture, accompanied by political repressions. The official ideology of the country was building Communism. Stalin ruled Russia until his death in 1953.

of European Russia, threatening Moscow and besieging Leningrad — as St Petersburg was known in the Soviet period. One million people died from hunger, bombing or military action during the nine-hundred-day Siege of Leningrad. The Germans failed in their deliberate attempts to raze this beautiful city from the face of the earth.

41. *Storming the Winter Palace.*
    Artist V. A. Kuznetsov
42. *Vladimir Lenin in 1918.*
    Artist Victor Tsyplakov
43. Red Army soldiers
44. "Ilyich (Lenin) lamps"
    or bringing electricity
    to a Russian village
45. Writer Maxim Gorky
    (Alexei Peshkov)
46. Physiologist Ivan Pavlov
47. Opera singer Fedor Chaliapin

45

46

47

48

49

50

48. Film director Sergei Eisenstein
49. *Morning of the Five-Year Plan. Constructing the Magnitogorsk Metallurgical Works.* Artist Jacob Romas
50. Constructing the Dnieper Hydro-Electric Power Station — the largest of its kind in the pre-war Soviet Union
51. "For the Motherland and Stalin!" Battalion commander leading soldiers into attack
52. *Defence of Sebastopole.* Artist Alexander Deineka

Russia has always produced men of genius. The scientists Ivan Pavlov, Pyotr Kapitsa, Abram Joffe and Igor Kurchatov, the writers Maxim Gorky, Mikhail Sholokhov and Andrei Platonov, the film directors Sergei Eisenstein and Vsyevolod Pudovkin and the composers Dmitry Shostakovich and Sergei Prokofiev were active in the 1920s and 1930s.

The Second World War brought more suffering to the Russian lands. Industrial and agricultural destruction was catastrophic. After the initial shock, the country began to fight back. Led by such talented commanders as Georgy Zhukov, Alexander Vasilyevsky, Konstantin Rokossovsky and Nikolai Vatutin, the Red Army expelled the Nazi invaders. The Russians pursued the Germans all the way to Berlin, liberating other nations in the process. Victory Day (9 May) was established as one of the most important public holidays.

Russia had to rebuild the country after the war. Many towns lay in ruins and more than twenty million citizens were dead.

53. Winston Churchill, Theodore Roosevelt and Joseph Stalin at the Yalta conference. February 1945
54. Soviet soldiers raising the victory banner above the Reichstag. 30 April 1945
55. Greeting soldiers returning home to the Bielorussky (White Russian) Railway Station in Moscow. 1945
56. Laying captured Nazi banners at the Lenin Mausoleum during the victory parade on Red Square. 24 June 1945
57. *Glory to Stalin the Great!* Artists Yury Kugach, Vasily Nechitailo and Victor Tsyplakov
58. Composers Sergei Prokofiev, Dmitry Shostakovich and Aram Khachaturian. 1940s

The problems of post-war reconstruction were exacerbated by the start of the Cold War. Threatened by the United States and Western Europe, Russia was obliged to spend large sums of money on arms and military technology. With incredible effort, Russia quickly restored its shattered economy and became one of the leading nations in terms of industrial production. Soviet scientists developed new weapons designed to maintain the balance of power.

In the late 1950s, Russia led the world in the exploration of space. The Soviet Union launched the world's first artificial satellite or "sputnik" on October 4, 1957. The man responsible for *Sputnik*, Sergei Pavlovich Korolyov, was a dominant figure in the spectacular first decades of the USSR's space-exploration effort. Then a number of unmanned spaceships of various kinds, ranging from meteorological and communications satellites to lunar probes were

59

59. Coat of arms of the Union of Soviet Socialist Republics
60. Pobeda — first post-war saloon car
61. Atomic-powered icebreaker *Taimyr*
62. Fidel Castro and Nikita Khruschev. Early 1960s
63. Writer Mikhail Sholokhov
64. Rocket engineer and designer Sergei Korolyov
65. Launch of a space rocket
66. First artificial earth satellite, launched on 4 October 1957
67. Yury Gagarin, the world's first cosmonaut
68. Parade on Red Square during the Soviet period
69. Soviet forces in Afghanistan
70. Meeting of the Politburo. Late 1970s

60 61 62 63 64

65 66 67

launched. On April 12, 1961, Yury Gagarin became the first man in space. Russia is proud of its achievements in the conquest of outer space. On March 18, 1965, Aleksey Leonov became the first man to float free in space. The "Vostok" spacecraft enabled the preparation of new, more complicated flights. There were 40 "Soyuz" spaceships launched between 1967 and 1981. "Salyut-1", launched in 1971, was the world's first space station. The first record for the longest manned mission in spaceflight history was set in 1981 by the crew of "Soyuz-35". It remained on board "Salyut-6" for 185 days. In 1986 the Soviet Union launched a more advanced type of space station "Mir".

The centralisation of the economy and planned system did not allow the country to develop. Stagnation pervaded all aspects of Soviet life. In December 1991, the USSR ceased to exist. Each of the fifteen Soviet republics became an independent country.

Russia embarked on a period of radical capitalist reforms. Fresh problems appeared in the form of economic instability, interethnic conflicts, corruption and criminal authorities. The absence of a national

71. Symbol of the Moscow Olympics. 1980
72. Mikhail Gorbachev and Ronald
    Reagan. Second half of the 1980s
73. Academician Andrei Sakharov
    at the Kremlin Palace
    of Congresses. 1990
74. Events in Moscow in August 1991
75. Boris Yeltsin, first president
    of the Russian Federation. 1990s

idea contributed to the disintegration of society. The concentration of wealth in the hands of a few oligarchs, the impoverishment of a large part of the population and the absence of a middle class threatened the continued existence of the country in the 1990s. Hope for an improvement in life appeared at the start of the new millennium. The country remained intact and signs of economic stability began to emerge. Once again, the Russian nation promises to emerge from a difficult situation with honour. There are many reasons for optimism. Russia is rich in natural resources, with large reserves of iron, nickel, aluminium and other metal ores, coal, oil, natural gas, tungsten, molybdenum, mercury and gold. The mechanical, construction, fuel, energy, metallurgical, agricultural, industrial, transport and military complexes contribute to the national economic wealth. The chemical, timber, light, food and electric industries are also well developed.

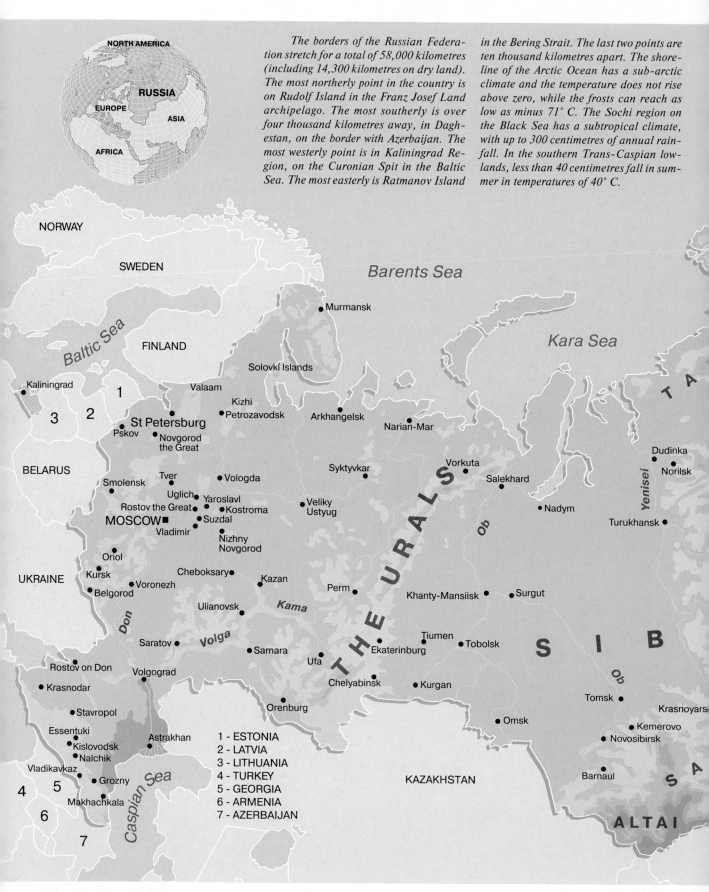

The borders of the Russian Federation stretch for a total of 58,000 kilometres (including 14,300 kilometres on dry land). The most northerly point in the country is on Rudolf Island in the Franz Josef Land archipelago. The most southerly is over four thousand kilometres away, in Daghestan, on the border with Azerbaijan. The most westerly point is in Kaliningrad Region, on the Curonian Spit in the Baltic Sea. The most easterly is Ratmanov Island in the Bering Strait. The last two points are ten thousand kilometres apart. The shoreline of the Arctic Ocean has a sub-arctic climate and the temperature does not rise above zero, while the frosts can reach as low as minus 71° C. The Sochi region on the Black Sea has a subtropical climate, with up to 300 centimetres of annual rainfall. In the southern Trans-Caspian lowlands, less than 40 centimetres fall in summer in temperatures of 40° C.

NORTH AMERICA

RUSSIA

EUROPE

ASIA

AFRICA

NORWAY

SWEDEN

Barents Sea

Kara Sea

Murmansk

Baltic Sea

FINLAND

Solovkí Islands

Valaam

Kizhi

Kaliningrad

1

Petrozavodsk

Arkhangelsk

Narian-Mar

T A

3   2

St Petersburg

Pskov   Novgorod
         the Great

BELARUS

Smolensk   Tver

Vologda

Syktyvkar

Vorkuta

Salekhard

Dudinka

Norilsk

Yenisei

Uglich   Yaroslavl

Rostov the Great   Kostroma

Veliky
Ustyug

Nadym

Turukhansk

MOSCOW   Suzdal

Vladimir

Nizhny
Novgorod

Ob

THE URALS

Oriol

UKRAINE

Kursk

Voronezh

Belgorod

Cheboksary

Kazan

Perm

Khanty-Mansiisk

Surgut

S I B

Ulianovsk

Kama

Don

Saratov

Volga

Samara

Ufa

Tiumen

Ekaterinburg

Tobolsk

Ob

Rostov on Don

Volgograd

Chelyabinsk

Kurgan

Tomsk

Krasnoyars

Krasnodar

Orenburg

Omsk

Kemerovo

Stavropol

Novosibirsk

Essentuki

Astrakhan

1 - ESTONIA

KAZAKHSTAN

Kislovodsk

Nalchik

2 - LATVIA

3 - LITHUANIA

Barnaul

S

A

Vladikavkaz

4 - TURKEY

4   5   Grozny

5 - GEORGIA

Caspian Sea

6 - ARMENIA

Makhachkala

6

7 - AZERBAIJAN

ALTAI

7

ARCTIC OCEAN

Providenia

CHUKOTKA

East Siberian Sea

Pevek
Anadyr

Bering
Sea

Laptev Sea

Kolyma

Y R

KAMCHATKA

Tiksi

Lena

Khatanga

Verkhoyansk

Magadan

Petropavlovsk-
Kamchatsky

Y A K U T I A

Yakutsk

Sea
of Ojotsk

Tura

Lena

The Kuril Islands

R I A

Mirny

Sakhalin

Yuzhno-Sakhalinsk

Angara

Amur

MARITIME REGION

Bratsk

Khabarovsk

Blagoveschensk

Lake
Baikal

Chita

A N

Irkutsk

Ulan-Ude

CHINA

Vladivostok

Kyzyl

MONGOLIA

Sea
of Japan

JAPAN

MOSCOW –
CAPITAL OF RUSSIA

Moscow's stellar brilliance is symbolic of its historical role as the gatherer of the Russian lands, the first capital where princes and tsars were crowned in an act that lent legitimacy to the authority of the individual brought to the throne, be they the natural heir or another member of the ruling family. Moscow took root in the very heart of the Russian lands and gradually became immortal. Although it was repeatedly burned to the ground, it rose from the ashes each time like the phoenix.

77

78 79

For centuries Moscow has been a treasure house of carefully preserved national
tradition. All the Russian tsars and emperors were crowned here in Russia's main cathedral, the ancient Dormition Cathedral,
and both Peter the Great and Catherine the
Great came to Moscow to celebrate their
military victories. In 1812 the city was a sac-
rifice on the altar of the war, yet precipitat-
ed the inglorious demise of Napoleon's great
army. During World War II (1941–45) Moscow suffered a great deal. On December 6,
1941 a desperate counterattack threw the
Germans back from the outskirts and saved
Moscow. That was the first defeat of the
Nazis. After the war recovery was quick and
followed by further construction of new dis
tricts and annexation of outskirts and suburbs. Moscow with its satellites (outer Moscow) covers 1,000 km².

Moscow is a major scientific and cul-
tural centre. It boasts fine architectural en-
sembles including the Kremlin, the Donskoy
and St Simon monasteries, the Novodevichy
Convent and St Daniel's Monastery, the
residence of the Patriarch of Moscow and
All Russia who is the head of the Russian
Orthodox Church. Moscow is the seat of the
President and the government. The Federal
Assembly consisting of two chambers, the
State Duma and the Council of Federation,
has its sessions here.

The Kremlin is Moscow's central architectural ensemble, the heart of Russia and
symbol of her greatness. It is situated on the
high bank of the Moscow River, at the mouth
of the Neglinnaya (put into a conduit in the
course of sanitation work and the city centre reconstruction, in 1816–20). This is the
oldest part of Moscow, that as far back as
the 11th century was the site of the Slavian-

sky town and its first manuscript reference
dates from 1147. In the reign of Yury
Dolgoruky it was surrounded by a moat with
ramparts. In the early 14th century Moscow became capital of the principality with
the white-stone Kremlin developing into an
impregnable fortress.

Towards the end of the 15th century,
when the Moscow principality was transformed into the state of Muscovy, the Kremlin assumed a new significance, it was rebuilt and enlarged. It was then that the ensemble's style was mainly formed, its area of
27.5 hectares being enclosed with new
mighty fortified structures. Majestic new cathedrals replaced the former white-stone
churches on Sobornaya and Ivanovskaya

*The fortress walls have an overall
length of 2,235 m. Along the perimeter stand
eighteen fortified towers, with the Kutafya
Tower overlooking the Troitsky Bridge
across the River Neglinnaya. Faced with
large, well-baked bricks weighing 8 kg
each, the walls are from 5 to 19 m high de-
pending on the reilef detail, and from 3.5
to 6.5 m thick as far as the merlons.*

76. Kremlin Embankment
77. Ruby star
78. Kremlin Towers
79. Troitskaya and Kutafya Tower
80. Konstantino-Yeleninskaya,
    Nabatnaya and Spasskaya Towers.
    Hipped roofs added in the
    17th century

80

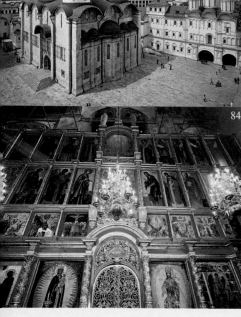

Squares, which now seemed too small, and the princes' and boyars' dwellings stretched from the slope of Borovitsky Hill to the western section of the fortified wall. This notable period of construction work was carried out by Italian architects invited to Russia by Ivan III. They included Aristotele Fioravanti, Alovisio di Carcanno, Marco Ruffo, Pietro Solario and Antonio Gilardi. The Italian masters succeeded in creating essentially Russian forms of church architecture that served as models for subsequent construction over the following two centuries. Further development of the Kremlin as an ideological, political and cultural centre was impelled by the growth and territorial expansion of the capital. Intensive building in the 17th century transformed the Kremilin, giving it the characteristics we see today. The Terem Palace and its churches, the Poteshny (Amusement) Palace (site of the first theatrical performances in Russia) and the Patriarch Courtyard with the Cathedral of the Twelve Apostles were erected, and the towers were

81. Cathedral of the Dormition. 1475—79. Architect Aristotele Fioravanti
82. Cathedral of the Dormition. Iconostasis of the cathedral. 1653
83. Cathedral of the Annunciation. 1485—89
84. Cathedral of the Archangel Michael. Iconostasis. 1679—81
85. Cathedral of the Archangel Michael. 1505—08. Architect Alovisio Novo

topped with many-tiered hipped roofs. In the 18th and 19th centuries major construction and reconstruction work was carried out in the palace complex and the state administration buildings: the Arsenal, Great Kremlin Palace, Senate and Armoury all date from the period. The best Russian architects participated in it – Bartolomeo Rastrelli, Nikolay Lvov, Vasily Bazhenov, Matvey Kazakov, Konstantin Thon and Carlo Rossi.

In the Soviet epoch the Monastery of the Miracle (Chudov) and the Ascension Monastery were demolished along with a great number of churches. The Palace of Congresses was built next to the Patriarch Palace between 1959 and 1961.

The fortified structures of the Moscow Kremlin are best examples of mediaeval European fortifications. They were erected between 1485 and 1495 by the Italian architects Marco Ruffo, Antonio Gilardi, Pietro Antonio and Alovisio Antonio Solario. Multitiered towers, originally crowned with flat platforms for accurate aim in the traditional manner of European fortresses, were elevated with the addition of tall hipped roofs

in the 17th century. They reach a height of 28 to 71 m, the Spasskaya (Saviour) and Troitskaya (Trinity) being the tallest. In 1505–08 a bell tower some 60 m high was put up above the existing Church of St John Climacus which was accordingly named in honour of the saint: "Ivan (John) the Great". In 1600 the tower was extended to a height of 81 m. The Church with the Bell Tower of the Resurection of Christ was added to the north flank between 1532 and 1534. It houses the largest bell in Russia still in working order — the Dormition, or Festive, Bell.

86. Cathedral of the Annunciation. View of the cathedral iconostasis. 1450
87. Domes of the Kremlin cathedrals
88. Religious service at the walls of the Dormition Cathedral
89. Faceted Palace. Red (Beautiful) Porch
90. Faceted Palace. Interior
91. Architectural ensemble with "Ivan the Great" bell tower. 1505–08, architect Bon Friazin; 1532–43, architect Petrok Maly; 1600, 1624, architect Bazhen Ogurtsov
92. Ivanovskaya Square. Tsar-Bell. 1733–35. Cast by I. and M. Motorin Master A. Chokhov
93. Ivanovskaya Square. Tsar-Cannon. 1586. Master A. Chokhov

91

94.

94. State Armoury. 1844—51. Architect
    K. Thon
95. Royal regalia of Russia
96. Attributes of a warrior in Old Russia
97. Banner with the Emblem of
    the Russian Empire. Royal sword,
    sheath and shield.
    Late 17th century. Moscow
98. Sabre in sheath. 1829. Master
    I. Bushuyev. Town of Zlatoust.
    Steel, bronze, wood and ivory;
    etching, casting, burnishing
    and gilding
99. Diamond Fund. Brooch. 1777.
    Diamonds, rubies, gold and silver
    Diadem: Russian Beauty. 1987.
    Diamonds, pearls and gold
    Brooch (holder for a small bouquet
    of flowers). C. 1770. Diamonds,
    emeralds and gold. Brooch.
    Second half of the 18th century

95.

96.

97.

98.

The State Armoury is the oldest museum in Russia since the collection was started by the grand princes of Muscovy in the 14th and 15th centuries long before the Armoury Palace itself was established. The Treasure House, the first depository for valuables, was built in the Kremlin in 1485. The Armoury is first mentioned in a chronicle dating from 1547. Originally it was used not only as a treasure house for valuable art objects but also as a workshop where both ceremonial and martial arms were produced. In addition to the armourers there were engravers, metalworkers, bone-carvers, gilders and filigreeworkers. In the 18th century production ceased, and towards the beginning of the 19th century the Armoury received the status of royal museum. Nowadays this is one of the finest collections of Russian and foreign decorative and applied art from the 4th to early 20th centuries. One of the most valuable pieces is the famous Monomachus cap, the crown of Russian tsars. According to legend the Monomachus cap was sent to the Russian grand prince by Byzantine Emperor

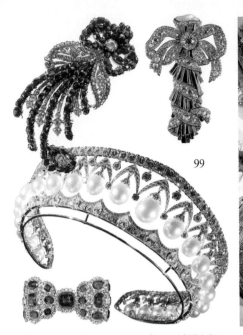

99

100 101

Constantine Monomachus. Since 1547 it has been used to crown the Russian tsars.

The State Armoury holds pieces by jewellers from St Petersburg's firm of Carl Fabergé. Its refined Easter eggs made the firm famous worldwide. Best samples of its production composed of precious stones and metals, decorated with ivory, mother-of-pearl and other materials are displayed in the museum.

The ground floor of the Armoury building houses the Diamond Fund of Russia established in 1922. Kept in it are unique precious stones and recognized masterpieces of the art of jewellery.

The earliest items date from the 1750s – 1760s. These are magnificent hairpins, earrings and diadems. They are adorned with diamonds of extraordinary brilliance. Of great historical and artistic value are the Great Imperial Regalia fashioned by Jérémie Pauzier in 1762 for the Coronation of Catherine II. This unique set is renowned for its fine craftsmanship and elegant design.

102

100. Orders and decorations from the Armoury and Diamond Fund
101. Double throne (of Tsars Ivan Alexeyevich and Peter Alexeyevich). 1682–84. Silver and wood
102. Easter egg commemorating the 300th anniversary of the Romanov dynasty. 1913. Carl Fabergé. Gold, enamel, ivory, diamonds and crystal.
Easter egg containing a model of the Alexander Palace. 1908. Carl Fabergé. Jade, gold, platinum, diamonds, rubies and enamel
103. Showcase with samples of Western European arms
104. Vessel in the shape of a horseman (equestrian portrait of Charles I). Before 1647. Augsburg, Germany. Gold and silver; chasing

103

104

The cathedral of the Intercession was built by order of Ivan the Terrible and with the blessing of Metropolitan Macarius. The cathedral was to commemorate an important event — the victory of the Russian army over the Kazan Khanate and final liberation from the Tartar-Mongol yoke, as a result of which the Russian lands were united round Moscow as their capital. The concept of a cathedral-monument brought forth the unusual architectural forms: nine churches are set on a lofty pedestal, eight of them are grouped round the central Church of the Intercession, whose hipped roof towers above the others at a height of 47.5 m. In 1588 the popular "fool for Christ" Vasily, or Basil the Blessed, was buried in the north-east corner of the cathedral. A tenth church dedicated to St Basil was added to the existing structure directly above his tomb, and since then the whole ensemble is commonly referred to as the Cathedral of St Basil the Blessed.

105

108

107

Throughout the history of Moscow Red Square has been integral part of the Kremlin ensemble. Its original name was Poloye ("waste") place, or Pozhar. Later it turned into the city's main market place known as Torg. In the 17th century it was given its present-day name of Red Square which means "beautiful" in Slavonic. The square has been the stage of most important events in Russian history. It witnessed long festive religious processions, royal trains and arrivals of foreign embassies. People crowded here to listen to the royal edicts that were proclaimed from Lobnoye Mesto ("place of a skull") — a circular platform faced with stone slabs. Lobnoye Mesto was also the site of public prayers and executions.

In 1612 the Russian army led by Kuzma Minin and Dmitry Pozharsky marched through Red Square to the Kremlin to drive the Poles out. To commemorate the event the monument to Minin and Pozharsky was set up here in 1818. In 1812 Napoleon inspected his troops on the square, yet soon suffered a crushing defeat. In 1945 after the end of World War II, the Victory Parade was held on Red Square, with soldiers from all the fronts taking part. In its architectural perfection and beauty Red Square can rival the most famous squares in the world.

105, 108. Panoramic view of Red Square and the Kremlin
106. Red Square. Cathedral of St Basil the Blessed. 1555—61. Architects Barma and Postnik
107. Guard in a 17th-century costume
109, 111. Red Square. Mausoleum of Vladimir Lenin (1930. Architect A. Shchusev) and the Sarcophagus containing the body of Lenin
110. Red Square. Feast Soviet day
112, 113. Alexander Garden. Eternal flame at the Tomb of the Unknown Soldier and the Guards of Honour

114 115

The Bolshoi Theatre has been famous for its brilliant singers, dancers, conductors and stage-set artists. Such names as Fedor Chaliapin, Leonid Sobinov, Antonina Nezhdanova, Yekaterina Geltser, Sergei Rachmaninov and Konstantin Korovin are the pride of both Russian and world musical culture. Among the company's best productions are operas Boris Godunov, Khovanshchina, Sadko, War and Peace, Othello, Aida, Don Carlos *and ballets* The Fountain of Bakhchisarai, Swan Lake, Nutcracker, Romeo and Juliet, Spartak *and many others.*

After the victory over Napoleon in 1812 and after the catastrophic retreat of the French troops Moscow was rapidly restored and rebuilt. In 1817 a new plan for the development of the ancient capital was introduced by the specially organized Construction Committee. It launched a great program of rebuilding, which included a partial replanning of the city centre. The Russian architect Osip Bove played a big part in its work.

Located on the opposite side of the Kitay-gorod wall in the middle of Theatre Square is the Bolshoi (Petrovsky) Theatre.

The edifice decorated with a monumental eight-column portico emphasizes the main axis of the square. Also on Theatre Square is the Maly (Little) Theatre.

The building of the Bolshoi Theatre is one of the best examples of Russian architecture from the mid-19th century and a largest theatre structure in Europe. It is the leading opera house of the country. Staged here have been operas by Mikhail Glinka, Modest Mussorgsky, Alexander Borodin, Nikolai Rimsky-Korsakov, operas and ballets by Peter Tchaikovsky.

116

117

118

Tverskaya (in the Soviet period Gorky) Street is the main street of Moscow. Known since the 14th century it became the city's major thoroughfare in the 15th – 17th centuries when relations with north-western Russian principalities, primarily Tver and Novgorod, began to play an important part in Moscow's economy. Another impact was given to its development in the 18th century when the new capital of St Petersburg was founded in the north. It was Tverskaya Street that all who came to Moscow from St Petersburg and vice versa travelled along. Though the street might be greatly changed, it retained its representative character. It was wider and busier and looked more ceremonial than other streets. In accordance with the Soviet plan for Moscow's reconstruction Gorky Street was the first to undergo certain improvements. Some of its buildings were demolished, others moved to other sites as a result of which the street became 2.5 times wider, thus the architects emphasized its leading role among other streets.

Tverskaya Street links several squares. Pushkin (former Strastnaya) Square, though much altered, better than others answers its original purpose of public square. The history of another square is no less complicated. It came into existence in the late 18th century when it was designed by M. Kazakov as a drill ground in front of the Moscow Governor-General house. In the second half of the 1930s it was widened and built with multi-storeyed houses, thus assuming more austere and ceremonial character to match the style of the Moscow City Council Office (where the city authorities sit now) that stands in it.

114. Bolshoi Theatre. S. Zakharova.
     Swan Lake by Peter Tchaikovsky
115. Bolshoi Theatre. Auditorium
116. Apollo's chariot atop the Bolshoi
     Theatre building. 1856
117. *Prince Igor* by Alexander Borodin
118. Bolshoi Theatre. 1821—24,
     architects O. Bove and A. Mikhailov;
     1855—56, architect A. Cavos.
     Sculptor P. von Klodt
119. Monument to Alexander Pushkin.
     1880. Sculptor A. Opekushin
120. Tverskaya Street. Former
     Yeliseyevs' food shop
121. Tverskaya Square. Office
     of the Moscow Government.
     Monument to Prince Yury
     Dolgoruky. 1954
122, 123. Tverskaya Street

124, 125. State Pushkin Museum
of Fine Arts. Italian courtyard:
one of the museum rooms.
Main staircase

126. Giovanni Antonio Boltraffio.
St Sebastian. C. 1500

127. Lucas Cranach. 1472–1553
Madonna and the Child

128. Pierre-Auguste Renoir.
Girls in Black. Early 1880s

129. Pablo Picasso.
Girl on a Ball. 1905

130. Edgar Degas.
Blue Dancers. C. 1898

131. Paul Gauguin.
Are you jealous? 1892

132. Andrei Rublev.
Icon of the Holy Trinity. 1410s

124

125

The world-famous Museum of Fine Arts is a major centre for the study of Western European art in Russia, second only in importance and scope to the renowned Hermitage in St Petersburg. The idea of creating a collection within the fine art and antiquities department of Moscow University which would cover all periods in the development of world art history and above all act as an educational institution received public approval in the mid-19th century. The new museum was financed by leading Moscow patrons of arts: noblemen, industrialists and merchants. The building assumed the form of a Greek temple on a high podium, with a Ionic colonnade at the central facade. The first-floor rooms have glass ceilings designed by the well-known engineers I. Roehrberg and V. Shukhov. Expertise gained from the museums at Dresden and Berlin was used to create the new Moscow museum. Russian and foreign scholars were consulted to establish the purposes and programmes of the museum. The Museum of Fine Arts affiliated to Moscow University was opened on May 31, 1912. In the 1920s and 1930s the holdings increased considerably after nationalization of private art collections, reorganization of the Moscow Public and Rumyantsev Museums, the addition of collections from the country estates outside Moscow and the closure of the Ostroukhov

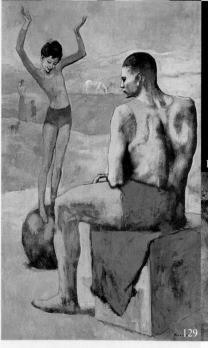

126

127

128

129

130

131

museums at the turn of the century were blessed with true foresight as a result of their passion for art, thorough knowledge and impeccable artistic taste. They discovered Post-Impressionism unrecognized even in Paris yet. Both collections were displayed in the owner's residence and open to the public. Several young artists who came to view the exhibits later became world-famous representatives of the Russian avant garde.

The Tretyakov Gallery is one of the most famous art museums in the world. Its collection covers a whole millennium of Russian cultural development. The founder was a Moscow merchant and industrialist who was also a great art expert, connoisseur and renowned patron: Pavel Tretyakov. In 1860 he wrote in his bequest: "I would like to form a national gallery collection comprising only paintings by Russian artists," which he devoted his entire life to. Every year he added what he considered to be the finest works of art to the gallery, buying paintings directly from the artists, their studios or exhibitions. Tretyakov's interests were wide-ranging. His collection presented Russian art in all its variety and historical development. It included not only pictures by contemporary artists but also works from the 18th – 19th centuries, as well as specimens of early Russian icon-painting. Originally they were displayed in the mansion of the Tretyakovs in Lavrushinsky Lane, the district of Zamoskvorechye. The collection had greatly expanded by the 1870s and for the following twenty years the owners had to build several new structures for its exhibitions. The famous colourful facade uniting the entire complex of buildings was erected after the death of Tretyakov between 1901 and 1903, to a design by eminent Russian artist V. Vasnetsov. This Russian-style structure is a symbol of national art.

Museum of Painting and Icon-painting. Later the museum received unique exhibits from the former Museum of New Western Art – the collections of S. Shchukin and I. Morozov. These two major Moscow collectors who had created their own private

133. *St George Slaying the Dragon.*
      First quarter of the 16th century
134. Ivan Shishkin.
      Morning in a Pine Forest. 1889
135. Victor Vasnetsov. *Bogatyrs.* 1898
136. Vasily Perov. *Hunters at Rest.* 1871
137. State Tretyakov Gallery. 1901—03.
      Facade designed by V. Vasnetsov
138. Kuzma Petrov-Vodkin.
      Bathing the Red Horse. 1912

The Cathedral of Christ the Saviour is situated in the city centre, not far from the Kremlin, on the high bank of the Moscow River (Kropotkinskaya Embankment). Built in commemoration of a great event in Russian history — the glorious victory over Napoleon's army in 1812, the structure was to be in accord with the architectural composition of the nearby Kremlin, Moscow's historical centre, and was modelled on the Kremlin cathedrals of the Dormition and the Archangel Michael. Its size is enormous: it is 103 m high, its area 6,805 m², the central dome's diameter 25.5 m. Construction of this grandiose edifice which could accommodate 10,000 people went on for dozens of years. The foundation was laid in 1839, the construction work completed in the 1880s and the consecration of the cathedral took place in 1889 after which daily services began there. The cathedral was lavishly decorated. A marble band with bas-reliefs showing Biblical scenes ran along the facades, above the portals. In 1931 the cathedral was exploded, later a swimming pool opened on the site. In the 1990s donations were made by thousands of people from all over the country and the cathedral was completely reconstructed on the original site. It looks exactly like the original structure, though the latest methods and materials have been applied. In January 2000 it was consecrated and opened for daily services.

139

140 /141

142

Numerous fires devastated Moscow in the past when most of its buildings were wooden. The 14th-century chronicle mentions "six great fires" which burnt the city to ashes. Moscow was also greatly damaged by foreign invaders. Most of the churches were stone so they could withstand both fires and invaders. In one of the oldest parts of Moscow, Khamovniky, a few ancient buildings including the Church of St Nicholas have survived. In the 17th century there used to be water meadows owned by the grand prince. Soon *khamovniki*, court weavers, were settled here, hence the name of the district. They built the Church of St Nicholas and decorated it with three tiers of *kokoshniks* (semicircular false gables) and bright multi-coloured tiles. Its elegant bell tower topped with a hipped roof is of special note. It has a lacelike pattern due to the numerous openings which make the acoustics better.

The Novodevichy Convent, one of the most beautiful monastic ensembles in Russia, has been a branch of the State Historical Museum since 1934. It was founded by order of Prince Vasily III in 1524, to commemorate the 1514 victory of Russia over

144

143

145

the Polish and Lithuanian forces in the battle for the borderlands and the return of the town of Smolensk. Situated near the road leading to Moscow from the south, it served as a military outpost on more than one occasion. The convent was favoured by the tsars and boyars, since the nuns included members of both royal and high-ranking families. The architectural ensemble was formed from the 16th to 17th centuries. The ancient convent cathedral was dedicated to the Smolensk icon of the Mother of God coming from Byzantium. It was a mostly revered icon in the Smolensk Province.

The State Historical, Architectural and Landscape Museum of Kolomenskoye is located in the south of Moscow. Kolomenskoye was particularly important during the reign of Ivan the Terrible and Alexey Mikhailovich. The unique architectural ensemble was built at this period. The dominant structure at Kolomenskoye is the Church of the Ascension. In the 16th century it served as a summer church for the tsar's family. It was erected to mark a momentous event – the birth of a long-awaited heir to the Russian throne, the future Ivan IV, called Ivan the Terrible. The church reaches a height of 62 m.

146

139. Cathedral of Christ the Saviour.
140, 141. Veneration of the Tikhvin icon of the Mother of God. 2004
142. Interior of the Cathedral
143. Novodevichy Convent
144. Church of St Nicholas at Khamovniky. 1679—82
145. Cathedral of the Saviour in the Andronikov Monastery. 1410—27
146. Kolomenskoye. Church of the Ascension. 1532. Feast day
147. Victory Memorial dedicated to Russia's victory in the Great Patriotic War of 1941—45 on Poklonnaya Hill. Church of St George. 1994—95

147

From the second half of the 1930s to 1950s a great number of buildings that can boast perfect artistic quality were constructed in Moscow. The architectural trend once labelled as "excessive embellishment" is no longer condemned. It is considered to be the Neo-Classical style now. At that time the architects were eager to create ensembles that would be in harmony with their elevated, triumphant mood and represent the ideals of the epoch. They were deliberate in using sumptuous, imposing forms. Such ensembles appeared in Tverskaya (former Gorky) Street and part of Kutuzovsky Prospect reconstructed before the 1950s. Most important architectural complexes to be created all over Moscow at the period

The buildings of Moscow University, different ministries on Smolenskaya and Komsomolskaya, Krasnye Vorota Squares as well as dwelling houses on Kotelnicheskaya Embankment and Vosstaniya Square added some new features to Moscow's outline, creating new vertical lines round which many districts' compositions were grouped and which were perceived as the components of the one grandiose plan.

148. Smolenskaya Square
149. View of Moscow taken from the Office of the Ministry of Foreign Affairs
150. Ukraine Hotel. 1956. Architects A. Mordvinov, V. Oltarzhevsky and V. Kalish

were the standardized high-rise buildings erected in commemoration of the 800th anniversary of Moscow and metro stations.

Moscow's metro stations called the "underground palaces" of Moscow are another attraction of the city. Used in their decoration are more than twenty varieties of marble coming from the Urals, Altai, Central Asia, the Caucases and Ukraine as well as labradorite, granite, porphyry, rhodonite, onyx and other natural stones. The magnificent, festive-looking halls and vestibules are adorned with sculpture, bas-reliefs, mosaics, paintings, stained glass panels and murals executed by the best artists. The Moscow underground was designed and built by eminent Soviet architects who aimed not only at utility and comfort but gave every station a unique look. The metro station *Mayakovskaya* opened in 1938 is considered one of the most beautiful. Its underground vestibule is supported by metal columns faced with granite and stainless steel. Mosaics in the cupolas were made after the sketches of A. Deineka.

In 1937 the *Mayakovskaya* station was awarded the Grand Prix at the World Fair in Paris as the first deep underground station supported with columns. At the same exhibition Moscow's metro stations of the first line were given a prize for perfect urban design. The first metro line began to operate in Moscow on May 15, 1935. New stations built nowadays are of simple and austere design.

153

THE MOSCOW METRO

154

151. High-rise building in Kudrinskaya Square. 1950—54. Architects M. Posokhin and A. Mndoyants
152. Main building of Moscow State University on Vorobyovy Hills. 1949—53. Architects L. Rudnev, S. Chernyshev, P. Abrosimov and A. Khryakov
153. *Ploshchad Revolutsii*. 1938. Architect A. Dushkin. Some of the metro stations are protected by the state as national property.
154. Plan of the Moscow metro
155. *Komsomolskaya-Koltsevaya*. 1952. Architects A. Shchusev, V. Kakorin and A. Zabolotskaya
156. *Park Pobedy*. 2003. Architects M. Bubnov and V. Nikolayeva
157. The Metrobridge on the Smolenskaya Embankment. 1937. Architects K. and Yu. Yakovlev

155

156

157

The New Arbat Prospect between Arbat Square and Sadovoye (Garden) Ring is another sight of present-day Moscow. The project worked out by a team of architects was awarded the Grand Prix by the Paris Centre of Architectural Research in 1966 for the renewal of architectural forms and achievements in working out long-term construction projects. The super modern style of this thoroughfare is made up by the geometrical regularity of its lines and the obvious repetitions and sharp contrasts of the forms. The verticals of the twenty-six-storey tower-shaped blocks rhythmically alternate with the lower, somewhat flattened, rectangular buildings that house cafes, bars, restaurants (including the *Tropicana* and *Metelitsa*) and

Modern Moscow keeps on rapidly building dwelling houses and public structures, both in its centre and suburbs. New problems arise that had to be solved due to the very heavy traffic. One of the main projects is the construction of the third city "ring" (circular road). Moscow has been recently adorned with many new and restored old Christian Orthodox churches. New architectural forms have enriched the Moscow scenery. Many foot-bridges have been recently constructed.

158. Panoramic view of Manège Square
     and the Kremlin walls
159. WWII veteran
160, 162. Best time of life
161. New Arbat. 1963–68. Architects
     M. Posokhin, A. Mndoyants, B. Thor,
     G. Makarevich, Sh. Airapetov,
     I. Pokrovsky, Yu. Popov, A. Zaitsev

shops (including the *Novoarbatsky*, one of the largest supermarket in the capital).

The light-coloured twenty-storey building that rises above Krasnopresnenskaya Embankment is known as the White House, as it is the seat of Russia's government. Its design is rather peculiar. The building consists of two parts. Above the lower seven-storey part with the side-wings there rises the narrower and taller part crowned by a small tower with a clock and the Russian Federation flag. A broad staircase leads up to the entrance, in front of which there is a wide square. Before designing the edifice the author headed a group of architects who created

166

the Russia Hotel, the largest in Moscow. Moscow is a major tourist and business centre. Many comfortable hotels coming up to the highest standards have recently been erected here. The Cosmos Hotel which can accommodate 3,600 people ranks among the hotels of the first international class. Located opposite the *VDNKh* metro station, in Mira (Peace) Prospect, the building was designed by Russian and French architects and engineers and constructed by a French firm. The upper part of this very tall structure comprising twenty-seven storeys has the shape of a cemi-cylinder. It forms a sort of mighty axis oriented towards the complex of the former Exhibition of Economic Achievements. Its facades are very impressive: their smoky goldish colour is created by the combination of the anodized aluminium of the walls and the dark-coloured glass of the windows and demonstrates a high quality of both construction and decoration work. The hotel has a well-equipped conference hall, a transformable banqueting hall, restaurants, cafes, bars, buffets, a swimming pool with a "beach" terrace, saunas and a bowling alley.

163. Ostankino TV-tower. 1960—67. Engineer N. Nikitin, architects L. Batalova and D. Burdina
164. Monument to Peter I. 1997. Sculptor Z. Tsereteli
165. On the Moscow highway
166. Bogdan Khmelnitsky Bridge. 2002. Architect Yu. Platonov
167. View of the Office of the Russian Federation Government on the Krasnopresnenskaya Embankment and Bagrationovsky Bridge
168. Bagrationovsky Bridge. 2000. Architect Yu. Platonov

167

168

GOLDEN RING

The Golden Ring is a tourist route running through a series of cities and towns in central Russia, which are remarkable for their ancient history and abundance of historical and cultural monuments. The area they occupy became the centre of Russia in the twelfth century. The steadily growing pressure of the nomads from the southern steppes resulted in a large-scale migration of the population to the north-east, to the lands of the Vladimir-Suzdal Principality, where dense woods provided protection from the steppe cavalry. The cities of the Golden Ring were also important points on the trade routes between the North and the South, Europe and Asia.

169

170

171

Sergiev Posad does not rank among the oldest towns of the Golden Ring, but it occupies an exceptionally prominent place in Russian culture and history. The very name of the town, meaning Sergius's Settlement, has a profound sense it is associated with Russia's most brilliant spiritual leader St Sergius of Radonezh, the saint of the Orthodox Church revered in Russia for many centuries. St Sergius founded in this area a secluded monastic abode. Soon the skete grew into a monastery and a settlement developed around it. The settlement gathered all sorts of people related to the life of the monastery, especially craftsmen, who laid the beginnings of some famous artistic handicrafts flourishing at Sergiev Posad and around it to this day. The picturesque complex of buildings of the Holy Trinity Monastery, or Laura, of St Sergius (laura is one of a few Russia's most important monasteries to which even the Tsars thought it honourable to make a pilgrimage on foot), which has organically blended with the lovely surrounding scenery, has been shaped in the course of several centuries. The earliest of its structures date back to the early Middle Ages, while one of the latest, the bell-tower, to the 18th century. The vertical of the Baroque bell-tower thrusting upwards does not clash with the whole.

The role of the monastery is associated not only with spiritual and religious problems but with general historical events, too. The monastery is skirted by the defensive walls, which were erected in the 16th and 17th centuries and proved their might several times. First of all, at the beginning of the seventeenth century, during the Time of Trouble, the Trinity–St Sergius Monastery withstood a siege by the army of the Polish-Lithuanian invaders. At the end of the seventeenth century the young Peter I took shelter within the walls of the laura twice.

The unquestionable authority of the founder of the monastery provided from the fourteenth century onwards an influx of the best intellectual and artistic forces, a flood of rich donations from noted statesmen and the richest families. The settlements of Sergiev Posad had many workshops of craftsmen who excelled in making crosses, ladles, silversmiths and other artistic objects. Thanks to all these factors the Treasury of the Holy Trinity Monastery of St Sergius and the State Museum of History and Art in Sergiev Posad possess unique collections of veritable treasures. Of especial interest among them are works by jewellers skilled in various techniques and pieces of embroidery.

169. Holy Trinity Monastery of St Sergius. The Cathedral of the Dormition (1559–85), the Chapel of St Paraskeva-over-the-Well (late 17th century), the burial vault of the Godunov family (1780) and the fountain pool (1872)

170. Icon depicting St Sergius of Radonezh. Ca 1424. Museum of History and Art, Sergiev Posad

171. Panoramic of the Holy Trinity Monastery of St Sergius

172. Holy Trinity Monastery of St Sergius. Bell-tower. 1740–70. Architects Johann Jacob Schumacher, Ivan Michurin and Dmitry Ukhtomsky

173. Holy Trinity Monastery of St Sergius. Cathedral of the Dormition. Interior

172

173

The Cathedral of the Holy Trinity (1422), much smaller than the Cathedral of the Assumption, is the spiritual and historical centre of the laura. The cathedral put up during the time of St Sergius suffered in 1408, during a fire in the monastery, a great damage. The present-day cathedral, built by St Sergius's successor, Hegumen Nikon, became the place where the holy relics of St Sergius are kept. It is also the place firmly associated in believers' notions with another Russian saint, the great artist

174

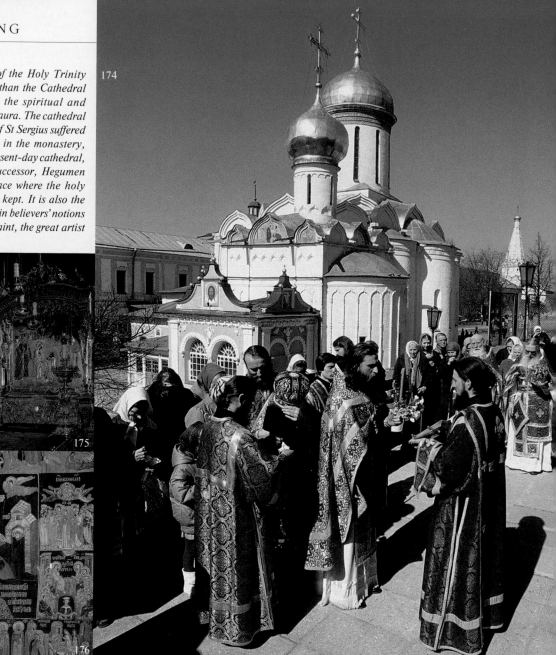

175

176

177

From the first years of its existence the monastery was the cultural centre where manuscript books were copied and talented writers worked, the most famous of which were Epiphany the Wise and Maxim the Greek. There are many first-rate architectural monuments at Sergiev Posad outside the laura, such as the Chapel of St Paraskeva-over-the-Well – a unique structure of the turn of the 17th and 18th centuries.

And still the most interesting buildings determining the image of Sergiev Posad can be found in its heart, the laura. The principal feature of the monastery ensemble is the bell-tower, which dominates the town as a whole and is visible even from beyond the towns borders. Its silhouette soaring to the height of more than eighty metres pro-

Andrei Rublev. The idea of unity and integrity embodied in the abstract form of the proportions and structures of the cathedral, is perfectly realized by means of painting in "The Trinity" by Andrei Rublev. This endows the Cathedral of the Holy Trinity, where the silver shrine containing the relics of St Sergius of Radonezh is kept, with a special significance of the earliest memorial church building in Russia. The shrine, an outstanding work of decorative art in its own right, was produced in 1585 by order of Ivan the Terrible.

duces an impression of lightness unusual for a structure of the advanced Baroque. The monastery was built in the course of several centuries. In the age of St Sergius the monastery was wooden and according to the available data, only the first Cathedral of the Holy Trinity that has not come down to us was built in stone. The largest structure of the complex is the Cathedral of the Dormition (1559–85) dedicated to the Mother of God especially revered in Russia. The building repeats in its basic proportions and constructions the Cathedral of the Assumption in the Moscow Kremlin that was the central cathedral of the Orthodox Church and was based, in turn, on the forms of the most ancient and highly prized Cathedral of the Dormition in Vladimir. By the north-western corner of the cathedral is situated the not very conspicuous burial vault of the Godunov family. By orders of the Pretender the body of Boris Godunov was taken out of the burial vault in the Cathedral of the Archangel Michael in the Kremlin and after being kept for some time in a Moscow monastery was transferred to the Holy Trinity Monastery of St Sergius that was patron-

ized and generously donated by Boris Godunov. In the second half of the nineteenth century, the merchant Riumin gave money for the construction, next to the Cathedral of the Dormition, of a canopied fountain pool. The shape of this structure is stylized in keeping with the notions of that time about the character of old Russian art.

The Church of the Holy Spirit (1476) plays a special role in the composition of the square standing in front of the cathedral it links the earlier structures with their austere and concise features and bright-coloured decorative structures of the 17th century.

Built at the end of the 15th century and modelled on the churches designed for the installation of bells over them, the Church of the Holy Spirit has elongated proportions in its upper tier for functional purposes. It embodies the most typical features of the Moscow Baroque: the plastic expressiveness of elaborate details and clear-cut ariculation of volumes. The chapel standing on the low land, at the foot of the hill dominated by the monastery, seems to meet travellers arriving from Moscow.

174. Festive day in the monastery
175. Cathedral of the Holy Trinity. Iconostasis and the shrine with the relics of St Sergius of Radonezh.
176. Shroud: The Appearance of the Mother of God to St Sergius of Radonezh. 1525
177. Mitre. Early 17th century. Phelonion. 1640–80. Gospel. 1754
178. Royal Chambers. Late 17th century
179. Cross. 17th century. Master craftsman Andrei Malov
180. Refectory with the church of St Sergius and St Micah
181. Interior of the refectory
182. Gateway Church of St John the Baptist. 1699
183. Interior of the church
184. Road among the fields →

185 186

185. Lake Nero. View of the St James
Monastery of Our Saviour
186. View of the walls, gateway church
and towers of the Rostov Kremlin
187. The Kremlin. Red or Fine
Chambers. 1670–80
188, 189. The fortress-like character
of the complex is a tribute to the
tradition of building monasteries
as fortified structures.
190. Interior of the Resurrection Church
191. Gateway Church of St John the
Divine. 1683

187

188

189　190

191　192

Rostov is one of the oldest Russian
towns. Favourable natural conditions attracted people to this area from time immemorial. The dramatic history of the town – internecine feuds of the principalities, the nomads'
incursions and the devastating Polish-Lithua-
nian-Swedish intervention of the early 17th century – gave to early historical monuments little chance for survival. But then in the 1630s
Rostov quickly flourished. Instead of the medieval town, practically erased by the invaders in 1608, a new ensemble, rather compact
in area and with a small number of buildings,
but strikingly integral and harmonious,
stretched in a picturesque way alongside
Lake Nero. The unique Rostov ensemble owes
much of its unity to the will and taste of one
man, who was destined to supervise the creation of this architectural masterpiece. Rostov gained its present-day appearance between 1660 and 1690, under Metropolitan
Jonah, an outstanding ecclesiastical figure and
one of the most educated men of his time.
The ensemble created under Jonah's supervision is in fact the metropolitan's court rather

193

195

194

196

198

199   200

197

192. The Kremlin. Cathedral
     of the Dormition (16th century)
     and the belfry (1682—87)
193. How the citizens of Rostov looked
     in the 17th century
194, 195. Of particular renown was the
     handicraft that developed in the
     18th century — the art of making
     filigree articles adorned with a fine
     enamel pattern over metal. Stalls
     with these vividly coloured objects
     became an original and indispens-
     able part of the urban scene.
196. The Trading Rows, the Church
     of Our Saviour-on-the-Marketplace
     and the Cathedral of the Dormition
197. Monastery of St James
198. The Rostov bell chimes won
     general renown as the most
     expressive in Russia.
199, 200. Monastery of St James.
     The inner yard and the octagonal
     tower of the fence

than a kremlin or citadel — the presence of mighty walls with battlements should not mislead us. As for practical defensive purposes, a system of walls was constructed on the ramparts, the remains of which are still visible in the town. A desire to attain the utmost outward effect of the ensemble is reflected in a whole number of absolutely original solutions in the design and decor of the buildings and certainly in the emergence of a distinct Rostov type of churches and fortress towers. The functional properties were part-ly realized in the towers: they had special places for watchmen, but the elaborate Baroque outlines of the tent-shaped tops certainly did not enhance the impression of stability and firmness. The two monasteries flanking the town — the Monastery of St James in the south-west and the Monastery of St Avraamy in the north-east — enhance the vivid impression produced by Rostov. They have common features in their design with the Metropolitan's Court — the Kremlin, as, for instance, the gateway churches with towers on either side.

Vladimir is one of the most ancient and beautiful cities of Russia. It was founded at the end of the tenth century by Prince Vladimir the Fair Sun or, according to another chronicle, by Vladimir Monomachus at the beginning of the twelfth century. In the middle of the twelfth century, under Andrew Bogoliubsky, Vladimir became the centre of North-Eastern Russia and later grew into the main city of the entire Russia. The position of Vladimir, lying on the high hills along the river valley, recalls that of Kiev located on the steep banks of the Dnieper. Moreover, the names of some rivers in the neighbourhood of Vladimir Lybed,

phase in the evolution of Russian white-stone architecture. The arrangement of the decor in many tiers reflects medieval cosmogonic notions. The Golden Gate with its monumental shapes is a fine example of medieval fortified structure. The gate is traditionally surmounted with a church that was supposed to protect the city both from the enemies and evil spirits. On the inner staircase wall of the gate visitors can see ancient graffiti: a sort of epitaph to Vladimir, son of Grand Prince Yury Dolgoruky, who died defending the city in the 13th century.

Bogolyubovo occupies a special place among other highlights of the Golden Ring. This is the only surviving complex, even if

201

The period of flowering of Vladimir's white-stone architecture, not long in terms of history, has left us a number of masterpieces of world significance, now on the UNESCO list. Founded by Grand Prince Andrei Bogoliubsky the Cathedral of the Dormition was for a long time the principal church of Old Russia. The perfection of its architectural image led to taking the cathedral in Vladimir as a model for a whole number of major Moscow churches. The surviving fragments of murals painted by the great Andrei Rublev and his closest assistant Daniel Chorny still further enhance the significance of the cathedral. Built a little later, the most beautiful church of Vladimir, Cathedral of St Demetrius marked the next

205

206

Irpen and Pochaina were directly borrowed from those in the Kiev region. The new all-Russian capital, a forerunner of Moscow and St Petersburg, originally was called Vladimir-on-the-Kliazma to differ the city from its southern namesake, Vladimir-Volynsky (of Volhynia). The Vladimir princes set themselves the task of building a city rivalling the beautiful Kiev in magnificence.

201. Bell-tower. 1810. Cathedral of the Dormition. 1158—60, 1185—89
202. Cathedral of the Dormition. Andrei Rublev. Fresco: The Last Judgement. 1408. Detail

with inevitable losses and alterations, that may be called a medieval castle. The castle-monastery stands on a hill at the edge of a river valley and the solitary Church of the Intercession can be seen nearby, on the low land, amidst water-meadows. Legend has it that the choice of the residence was foreordained in the heavens. During Prince Andrei's travel from the south to Rostov his horses carrying the miraculous icon the Mother of God stopped at the site where Bogolyubovo would be built. During the night the Virgin Mary appeared to the prince and promised Her heavenly patronage to him. The church was put up in honour of the new feast, the Intercession of the Virgin, established by the Prince of Vladimir and the city's priesthood without a sanction of the Metropolitan of Kiev. This feast symbolizing the protection of the Mother of God, was destined to become one of the most revered in Russia that was thought to be the earthly home of the Virgin. And it befell to the Church of the Intercession on the Nerl River to become a sort of symbol of Russian medieval culture.

207

208

209

210

211

212

203. Cathedral of the Dormition. Daniel Chorny. Fresco: The Last Judgement. 1408. Detail
204. Cathedral of the Dormition. Interior
205. The Golden Gate (1164)
206. Church of the Intercession on the Nerl. 1165
207, 208. Near Bogolyubovo
209. The Princess (Kniaginin) Convent of the Dormition (founded in 1200). View of the Dormition Cathedral
210. Panoramic view of Vladimir
211. Cathedral of St Demetrius. 1194—97
212. Detail of the facade of St Demetrius Cathedral

On 15 May 1591 Tsarevich Dmitry or Demetrius, son of Ivan the Terrible, the only heir to the crown, died in Uglich. Historians do not agree about the true reason of his death to this day. In any case, popular rumours accused Boris Godunov of being guilty of his death. Godunov, who soon became the Tsar of Russia, failed to win the true recognition of his power from the population.

226. The Kremlin. Church of St Demetrius-on-the-Blood. 1692
227. Church of St Demetrius-on-the-Blood. Of great interest is the destiny of the bell that warned the inhabitants of Uglich about

226

227

228

229   230

Uglich is located not far from Rostov. The first mention of the town in the chronicle dates from 1148. It is situated at the place where the Volga bed makes an abrupt turn, which probably gave its name to the town from "ugol" (angle). According to a different version, the town derived its name from charcoal-burning, which was a popular craft here (ugol meaning coal in Russian). There is a legend that even in the pre-Christian times the detachments of the Kievan princes used to come here to collect tribute. Uglich flourished in the 15th century when it minted its own coin and construction grew more active. At the end of the 16th century, when the Time of Troubles began, Uglich witnessed the tragic events, which largely determined the towns further destiny and left a dark imprint on entire Russian history.

During a mutiny at Uglich Boris's envoys were murdered, and the townspeople, who cherished to see the Tsarevich growing up next to them on the throne, refused to agree with the official explanation of the boy's death as an accident. The troops sent from Moscow meted out punishment to the mutinous population. Several years later the Polish-Lithuanian invaders met a fierce resistance at Uglich. The Uglich people would not accept the version declared by the Poles.

231

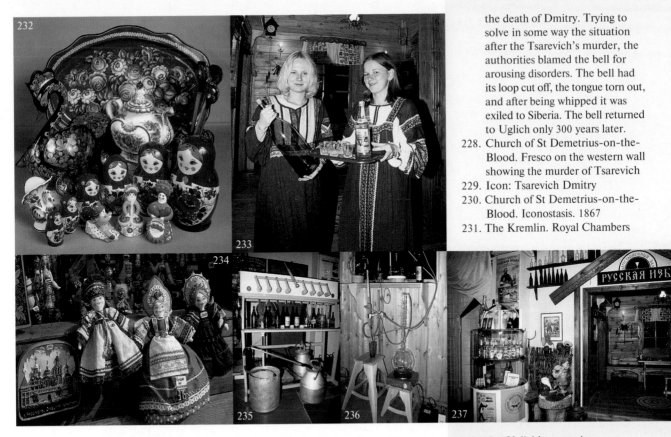

the death of Dmitry. Trying to solve in some way the situation after the Tsarevich's murder, the authorities blamed the bell for arousing disorders. The bell had its loop cut off, the tongue torn out, and after being whipped it was exiled to Siberia. The bell returned to Uglich only 300 years later.

228. Church of St Demetrius-on-the-Blood. Fresco on the western wall showing the murder of Tsarevich
229. Icon: Tsarevich Dmitry
230. Church of St Demetrius-on-the-Blood. Iconostasis. 1867
231. The Kremlin. Royal Chambers

The invaders wanted to put on the Russian throne the Pretender, who claimed to be Tsarevich Dmitry allegedly saved from killers sent by Boris Godunov. The town was ravaged and burnt down. At the spot where the Tsarevich had died a chapel was soon put up to be replaced over the years with the Church of St Demetrius-on-the-Blood, at first built in wood and later in stone. Bright colours and sumptuous relief decoration make this church the focal point of a panoramic sight from the Volga. The popular consciousness, however, has never lost its life-asserting quality. The radiant decor of the Church of St Demetrius-on-the-Blood convincingly proves that – as do the majestic look of the Cathedral of the Transfiguration and the festive appearance of the Church of

the Dormition in the Monastery of St Alexis, one of the first buildings constructed after the terrible Time of Troubles. The latter church, which became a memorial to the dead Uglich warriors, was aptly called Magnificent for its exclusively slender proportions and expressive decor. The relief details in the lower part of the structure are more restrained, yet even in this section the architects attained an expressive plastic solution.

232, 234. Uglich's souvenirs
233, 235–237. Museum of Vodka. The province of Uglich is the homeland of Pierre Smirnoff
238. Church of St Demetrius and the Cathedral of the Transfiguration
239. Monastery of St Alexius. Founded in 1371. Church of the Dormition (the Magnificent Church). 1628

238

239

The specific feature of Yaroslavl is that it was built up in a steady manner and there were no intervals in its construction from the eighteenth century onwards. The appearance of Yaroslavl is very organic in that the medieval, pre-Petrine buildings do not clash here with the contemporary housing construction based on the developed industry and modern infrastructure. Besides the famous landmarks of Old Russian architecture, worthy of special interest in Yaroslavl are also mansions and social buildings put up in the eighteenth to twentieth century, which reflect an evolution of styles in the past ages. The building of the local theatre (named after Fedor Volkov, a creator of the Russian professional theatre born in Yaroslavl) is a tribute to the Neo-Classical style of the early twentieth century. The elegant stylization of the Chapel of St Alexander Nevsky in the Russian style, a work of the late nineteenth century, was designated to emphasize the continuity of the past cultural traditions.

240. View from the belfry in the Monastery of Our Saviour
241. Monastery of Our Saviour. Founded in the 12th century
242. Monastery of Our Saviour. Holy Gates Tower (1516), the belfry (16th century), the Church of the Entry into Jerusalem (1617—19)

240

241

Yaroslavl is the largest and most urbanized city of the Golden Ring. It was founded at the spot where the Kotorosl River empties its waters into the Volga the place which seems to be destined by nature itself for the control of this important trade route. A legend associates its emergence with Yaroslav the Wise, one of the most outstanding rulers of Old Russia. This event is said to have taken place in the early 11th century. Yaroslav came to the bank of the Volga with his warriors and performed there the act that signified, in the eyes of the local pagans, the affirmation of a new invincible force he killed by his battle-axe the totemic She-Bear, the mother of the human race. It is perhaps due to this fact that the loyalty of the inhabitants of Yaroslavl, even during the age of the most ferocious feuds and troubles, to the power of the grand dukes. And the She-Bear holding an axe appeared on the scarlet field of the coat-of-arms of the Yaroslavl Princi-

242   243   244

pality. The city could recover after trials and tribulations. It suffered the greatest damage from the onslaught of the Mongol-Tartar hordes, and a terrible fire in the middle of the seventeenth century turned Yaroslavl into a desert covered with ashes. The energetic construction in the city after fires when every customer usually a settlement or a rich merchant (guest) sought to challenge his rivals in the perfection of the building under construction and as a result evolved a highly representative, Yaroslavl type of church. The Church of St John the Baptist at Tolchkovo appeared as a kind of structure typifying Yaroslavl architecture of the 17th century.

The Monastery of Our Saviour was the essential link in the urban ensemble of Yarosavl for many centuries. Various structures built in the course of several centuries were preserved there. The earliest of them dated from the early 16th century. These are the Cathedral of the Transfiguration and the Holy Gate with a watch tower. Incorporated into the system of urban fortifications, the monastery played the role of the most important fortification, too. Thus, in the early 17th century it successfully withstood the attacks of the Polish-Lithuanian invaders. It is no less important that the monastery was a major cultural centre: the first school in north-western Russia was opened in it.

245

246

247

and of the Yaroslavl Miracle-Workers (1827—31, architect P. Pankov), the Cathedral of the Transfiguration (1506—16)
243. Interior of the Cathedral of the Transfiguration
244. Beehives in the monastery
245. View of the Volga
246. The Kotorosl River. View of the Church of St John the Baptist at Tolchkovo
247. Chapel of St Alexander Nevsky. 1892. Architect N. Pozdeyev
248. The Korovniki Settlement. Church of the Icon of Our Lady of Vladimir (1669) and the Church of St John Chrysostom (1649—54)
249. Church of St John the Baptist at Tolchkovo. Detail
250. Church of the Prophet Elijah. 1647—50

248

249

250

The Church of the Resurrection-on-the-Debra stands out even among the richly decorated churches of Kostroma. Built simultaneously with the Cathedral of the Holy Trinity and similar to it in design, it is distinguished by a greater wealth and variety of details. The portal of its gate remarkable for its asymmetric design is adorned with relief representations of mythical creatures. A beautiful legend about the construction of the Church of the Resurrection-on-the-Debra has reached us. The merchant Cyril Isakov found a barrel of gold among the goods received from London in exchange for canvas. English businessmen informed their amazed partner that it was

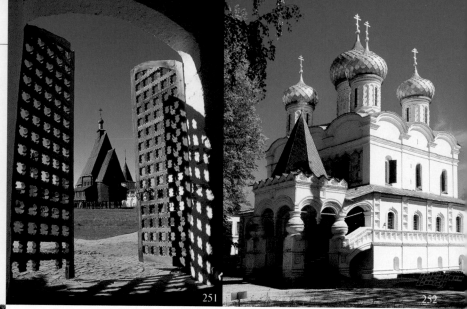

251

252

253

255

A little downstream the Volga from Yaroslavl lies Kostroma, a city the history of which is full of mysteries because ancient chronicles almost do not mention it. Some indirect records enabled Vasily Tatishchev, a noted eighteenth-century historian, to suppose that Prince Yury Dolgoruky founded Kostroma in 1152. Not participating in the struggle for leadership and having no ambitions to become the grand princes capital, this city won the glory of the linen capital of the north in the Middle Ages it produced the worlds best linen. It was not accidental that the coat-of-arms of Kostroma includes a golden ship with its sails filled out by the wind. Kostroma was a major trade centre of Russia and merchants from the greatest maritime state of the world, England, used to come here to purchase goods. The city, which stood at the outward bounds of the then cultivated lands, was not only engaged in trade, but also not infrequently served as a strategic point. It was in Kostroma that the grand princes Dmitry Donskoy in 1382 and his successor Vasily I in 1408 saved themselves during the Tartar-Mongol invasion. In the sixteenth century Kostroma was the point from which regiments set out for campaigns against the Kazan Khanate and in the 17th century False Dmitry tried to find shelter here from the Russian popular militia. The city was a temporary seat of Mikhail Fedorovich, the first Tsar of the Romanov Dynasty. In the winter of 1613, at the price of his own life, the peasant of the Kostroma district Ivan Susanin saved the Tsar from the Polish invaders.

254

to be used for a project pleasing to God. And they say that the merchant donated his money for the construction of this church.

251. Ipatyevsky Monastery (Monastery of St Hypatius). Carved gate
252. Ipatyevsky Monastery. Cathedral of the Holy Trinity. 1650—52
253. Chambers of the Romanov Family
254, 255. View of the Ipatyevsky Monastery (founded in the 1330s)
256. Church of the Resurrection-on-the-Debra. 1651
257. Fire alarm-tower. 1823—26. Architect P. Fursov. The alarm-tower became a major landmark in the central square and so the

The gem of the city's outskirts is the Ipatyevsky Monastery named after St Hypatius. The monastery spreads in a picturesque way along the bank of the Kostroma River not far from the place where it empties its waters in the Volga. The former monastery now houses the open-air Museum of History and Architecture famous for its rich collections. A variety of architectural motifs and observation points make this complex a unique tourist landmark. The monastery was founded in the 1330s by the former Tartar murza Chet who adopted the Orthodox faith. In the sixteenth century the monastery turned out to be connected with his descendants the influential Godunov family. The rich monastery with the family's burial place was to show that political ambitions of its patrons were well grounded. During the Time of Troubles the monastery buildings and defensive structures suffered a great damage. The present-day appearance of the Ipatyevsky Monastery took shape in the subsequent period. To the Old Town, which had existed as early as the fifteenth century, a plot of land was added in 1619 that was named later the New Town to contrast it with the earlier complex. The territory was marked with three towers, the middle one of which, the many-tiered Green Tower, became the main entrance to the monastery. Worthy of special interest among the early structures is the belfry of the late 16th century. The gateway Church of St Chrysanthus and St Darya blended well with the monas-

tery's complex completing it. The Gostiny Dvor or Trading Arcade was the heart of the marketplace. The strictly functional building opens up a series of civil structures of the late 18th and early 19th centuries. These magnificent buildings resolved in the Classicist style shape the centre of Kostroma.

main highways of the city, planned in a regular way after a fire of 1773, diverge in a fan-like manner from it.

258. Red or Fine Rows
     (Trading Arcade). 1789–1800
259. Pavilion on the Volga bank
260–263. Museum of Wooden Architecture

VOLGA, SOUTHERN RUSSIA, NORTHERN CAUCASUS

The French novelist Jules Verne who wrote about journeys and voyages and made them in his imagination compares the river Volga with a great tree whose branches (arms) reach to all parts of Russia. Numerous songs, folk tales, legends, poems and even novels are dedicated to the Volga. The Russians call it "the Mother Volga" or "bread-winner" and describe it as wide, mighty, glorious, great or sometimes calm and clear. The river unites different nations that have been living on its banks in peace for ages: the Russians, Tartars, Mari, Mordvin, Chuvash and even Germans (Volga Germans).

In the distant past oriental peoples called the great Russian river Ra and in the middle ages the name of the river was Itil. The modern name is a derivation from some Finno-Ugric language. It means "white" in the languages of Veps, Votic, Izhora (Ingra) and other nations inhabiting the Volga region for centuries, so the "Volga" can

264

265

266  267

269

A string of reservoirs built in the Soviet period line the Volga, among them Volzhskoye (the Moscow Sea), Uglich, Rybinsk and others. There are six hydroelectric stations. The river is joined by canals to the Baltic, White, Azov and Black Seas. It carries construction and raw materials, petroleum, foodstuffs (bread, fruits) and salt. The Uglich reservoir was formed by the dam of the hydroelectric station. Its lake which took the

268

270

be translated as *"a river with clear water"*. It is the continent's longest full-flowing river, 3,700 km long. Its basin, 1,360 km², sprawls across about two-fifth of the European part of Russia.

264, 265. The Volga source
266. Tolga Convent near Yaroslavl
267. Tutayev. Church of the Kazan Icon of the Mother of God
268. Kaliazin. Bell tower of St Nicholas's Cathedral-on-the-Zhabna. This part of the town was flooded after the construction of the Uglich lock.
269. Statue of the Volga River at the entrance to the Rybinsk lock
270. Leaving the Uglich lock
271, 274. On the Volga bank
272. Souvenirs made by local craftsmen
273. Folk festival in Tver Region

shape in 1939–41 covers 249 km², its volume is 1.25 km³. The reservoir supplies Uglich with water and has good fisheries. Situated in the same area are two smaller old towns: Kaliazin to the south of Uglich and Myshkin to the north, at the entrance to the Rybinsk reservoir. According to legend, the town of Myshkin was founded by a certain Myshkin who built the Dormition Cathedral in Moscow. Another legend tells that a local prince was sleeping on the Volga bank when a mouse chased by a snake woke him up and thus saved from probable death. He ordered to depict the small animal in the town's

emblem. The fact is that the name of Myshkin is a derivative of *"mysh"* which means "mouse" in Russian. This small town with a population of 6,500 has a charm of its own. Kaliazin is a river port on the Volga. It was founded in the 12th century at the confluence of the Zhabna and the Volga, on the right bank of the latter. After the construction of the Uglich hydroelectric station in 1937–40 a larger part of Kaliazin was flooded. Today it is a relatively small town situated on the Volga in the Tver province. Its population numbers 15,000. It produces *valenky* (traditional Russian felt boots) and linen articles.

271

272

273

274

275, 276. Nizhny Novgorod stands on the hight right bank of Volga

277, 278. Near Myshkin

279. The Kremlin of Kazan. 16th – 17th centuries

280. Volgograd. Memorial dedicated to the heroes of Stalingrad Battle on the Mamayev Kurgan (Hill)

281, 282. Nizhny Novgorod. River port

283. Samara. Roman catholic church

284. Samara. Railway station

285. Saratov. Church of the Icon of the Mother of God

286. Russian caviar was and remains the choicest delicacy and the best dish to treat a guest. The most tasty are unpressed black sturgeon caviar and the red caviar of the Far East salmon variety. "Caviar in boat-shaped crystal bowls, cooled in ice, white fish in parsley, all sorts of salmon, mounds of pressed caviar, mounds of cheese, a sturgeon gristle

275

276

277

278

The Volga has always been a major trading route connecting the north with the south. It is navigable from the town of Rzhev downstream. In the town of Tver it is 200 m wide. There are 40 cities and towns including Tver, Rybinsk, Yaroslavl, Kostroma, Nizhny Novgorod, Kazan, Ulianovsk, Cheboksary, Samara, Saratov, Volgograd (Stalingrad, Tsaritsyn before 1917) and Astrakhan as well as 1,000 smaller settlements on the Volga, most of which lie on the high right bank. Rising in the Valdai Hills, not far from Tver, it crosses the European part of Russia from north to south and discharges into the Caspian Sea. The river forms a wide delta, receiving the water of some 200 tributaries (long rivers, small streams and brooks). The Volga basin produces 25 % of all Russia's crops and one fifth of industrial fishing. The river contains 70 spe-

cies of fish, including 40 industrial (roach, herring, bream, pike-perch, wild carp, silurus, pike, sturgeon, sterlet and others).

Samara was founded in 1586 as a fortress at the confluence of the Samara and Volga rivers. In the 19th century it became a major trading centre, dealing in agricultural produce (particularly grain), linen and skins. Today the region is developing as a centre of car manufacturing, machinery and instrument making, the food industry, and other light industry.

Kazan, a port at the confluence of the Volga and Kazanka Rivers, is the capital of Tatarstan. It was the capital of the early Kazan khanate, which broke away from the Golden Horde and was annexed by Russia in the 16th century. It has a central kremlin, containing fortresses as well as both Islamic

279

280

281

282

283

284

285

in vinegar..." — this mouth-watering description by Ivan Shmelev, an émigré writer, gives some idea of the plentiful Moscow table on a festive day in prerevolutionary Russia. Caviar features prominently in this recollection and it really occupies a pride of place in the Russian cuisine.

In numerous taverns on the Volga, for example, they used to disembowel a just caught and still alive sturgeon in the presence of a guest, to season caviar with salt and to invite the guest to taste it right away. They used to eat caviar by tablespoons drinking vodka after that. Caviar served with hot *blinis*, eggs stuffed with caviar, caviar with finely minced onions and caviar served in large special bowls — all this was a common thing in Russia. Caviar was accompanied by icy champagne, chilled transparent vodka or strong hot and sweet tea.

286

and Orthodox shrines. The famous Kazan Mother of God icon is reputedly the source of miracles that have played a decisive role in the history of both imperial and contemporary Russia. Everyone in Russia knows the names of the Volga towns and cities that didn't surrender to the enemies in different periods of the country's history and where the enemies were routed. One of the decisive battles of World War II took place on the river, that was the battle of Stalingrad.

Astrakhan goes back to the 13th century. The city on the Volga delta boasts architectural landmarks from the 17th-century kremlin and the famous bazaars, filled with fruit, vegetables and fish.

"There it flows! Greetings, Don! From your distant brothers, I send a bow; Like a famous brother, Rivers know the quiet Don." Russian poet Alexander Pushkin understood the significance and character of the River Don — symbol of the vast hinterlands adjoining Russia from the south. The boundless steppes flanking the River Don have been inhabited ever since the Stone Age. It was home to the Cimmerians in the Bronze Age and, in the Stone Age, the Scythians and, later, the Sarmatians. There are many traces of ancient culture in the region. Such Greek scholars as historian Herodotus and geographer Strabonus have described the lives of its inhabitants. In 965, Prince Svyatoslav of Kiev defeated the Khazar khanate, who lived there. The battle took place on the bank of the River Don and is described in the famous Russian epic *The Tale of Igor's Host.*

288
289

287

290

291

292

Russia's southern borders were defended by the Cossacks, who also participated in all military campaigns. The first written records of Cossack settlements on the banks of the River Don date from the reign of Ivan the Terrible. "There is no extradition from the Don" was the law defining the free status of the Don Cossacks. Such rebellious atamans as Yermak Timofeyevich, Stepan Razin and Yemelian Pugachev brought fame to this land of freedom-loving people, distinguished for their wilfulness and great courage. In the early eighteenth century, Dutch admiral Cornelius Cruys wrote: "The Cossacks are good-natured and generous, do not amass wealth, have much intelligence, are crafty and particularly skilful in military affairs ... They are extremely brave, indifferent to hunger, thirst and all occurring rigours." The selfless service of the Russian state was historically ingrained in the Cossack consciousness. An émigré publication *The Path*

293

of the Cossacks (1928) claimed: "The Cossacks combined a burning love of their own lands with love for the common mother Russia ... The supreme Russian national idea was incontrovertible for the Cossacks."

One of the principal towns of southern Russia, Rostov-on-Don, arose in the eighteenth century as the fortress of St Demetrios of Rostov. The village of Starocherkasskaya and the town of Novocherkassk still contain monuments of culture and the structure of life of the Don Cossacks. In Russia, there were eleven Cossack hosts, including the Minor Host. Their homeland was the fertile soil, endless steppe, mountain ranges and seashores of the Kuban. The main towns were Krasnodar (a military camp in the eighteenth century) and Ekaterinodar (fortress of the Black Sea Cossacks). The unique climatic conditions of the Krasnodar region make it a popular place of relaxation for Russians.

287. Russian Cossack
288. Sunflowers
289. Grapes from Novorossiisk plantations
290. Kuban cow
291, 292. Rostov wheat
293. Picking winter apples in Krasnodar Region
294. Apple trees in blossom
295, 297. National fête in Rostov Region
296. Rostov-on-Don, River Don

The pearl of the Caucasus, the mineral waters region is located on the northern slopes of the Greater Caucasian Mountain Range, ninety kilometres from Mount El-brus, whose two-headed summit can be seen

298

The Greater Caucasian Mountain Range is partially located on the territory of the Russian Federation. This ridge stretches along the southern boundary of European Russia, between the Black Sea, Sea of Azov and Caspian Sea, from the River Kuma in the north to the border with Turkey and Iran in the south. The Russian part of the Caucasus includes Adygheya, Karachay-Cherkessia, Kabardino-Balkaria, North Ossetia, Ingushetia, Chechnya, Daghestan and Krasnodar and Stavropol Regions.

The Terek is one of the most famous Caucasian rivers. Tracing its descent from Georgia, it twists and turns through all the lands lying on its path. Besides Kabardino-Balkaria, the Terek flows through North Ossetia in two separate sections. It briefly serves as the border between Stavropole and the

299 300

throughout the entire region. It includes five towns — Mineralnye Vody, Pyatigorsk, Kislovodsk, Essentuki and Zheleznovodsk.

The health restorative properties of this unique, specially protected ecological region of the Russian Federation are without parallels in Eurasia. Over three hundred healing springs and numerous deposits of therapeutic mud are found here. The combination of beneficial climate, mineral waters and therapeutic mud means that all diseases of the human organs can be treated here.

The mineral waters region of the Caucasus is not only famed for its health restorative functions. It also has a rich

301

302

303

history and culture, indissolubly linked to the many famous people who once visited these places.

298. Vladikavkaz, North Ossetia
299. Nalchik, Kabardino-Balkaria
300. River Terek, Vladikavkaz, North Ossetia

Chechen republic, continuing its way through Chechnya, before finally entering Daghestan and falling into the Caspian Sea.

North Ossetia is a citadel of ancient culture. The Alans, who lived there approximately two thousand years ago, were known to the Ancient Romans. The Hermitage Museum in St Petersburg owns unique treasures of decorative and applied art found in the burial mounds of Alania. Dating from the fourth to sixth centuries, these masterpieces include works of gold, silver and bronze decorated with inlays. The Alans accepted Christianity and built extremely interesting churches. The earliest dates from the tenth century. The *Nart Epos* is a leading work of Alan literature. Ossetia and Kabardy were annexed by the Russian Empire in 1774, following the Treaty of Kucuk-Kaynarca ending the Russo-Turkish War.

Two Caucasian republics — Kabardino-Balkaria and Karachay-Cherkessia — lie at the foot of an extinct volcano. Mount Elbrus (18,506 feet) is the highest peak in Russia and Europe. Known as the "snow-capped mountain," it was extolled by Russian poets Alexander Pushkin and Mikhail Lermontov. On the territory of Kabardino-Balkaria, the northern slope of the Greater Caucasian Mountain Range is dotted with a series of summits, including Dykhtau and Shkhara, which are more than five thousand metres above sea level.

The nature of this land is stunning — age-old conifer forests, glacial lakes, tempestuous mountain rivers, picturesque ravines and healing springs. Architectural excavations prove that it was inhabited thousands of years ago, back in the Paleolithic period. The remnants of medieval and other

301. Isachenko Waterfall, Apsheron district, Krasnodar Region
302, 303. Adygheya landscapes
304. St Nicholas Cathedral, Kislovodsk
305. Narzan Gallery, Kislovodsk
306. Colonnade in Kislovodsk. 1912. Architect N.N. Semyonov
307. Kislovodsk Railway Station
308. Frogs Fountain, Kislovodsk
309. Glass Stream Pavilion, Kislovodsk
310. Kislovodsk Philharmonic. 1895
311. Fisht-Oshten Mountain Pass in the Caucasian Biosphere Reserve, Adygheya →

Adygheya is an enclave inside Krasnodar Region. Its name derives from the Adyghe people — native inhabitants of the Caucasus since Paleolithic times. The republic is famous for the Caucasian Biosphere Reserve, which is included in the UNESCO World Heritage List.

Lying in the west Caucasus, the reserve is home to a large number of rare plants and such endangered species as the bison, red deer, Caucasian goat, chamois and brown bear. The park has numerous caves, including the longest and deepest ones in Russia, forming complex underground systems of rivers, lakes and waterfalls. The Caucasian Biosphere Reserve boasts many mountain summits (over 11,000 feet), tempestuous and transparent mountain rivers and pure mountain lakes.

historical monuments — forts, castles, stone towers and mausoleums — still survive today. Inquisitive travellers are drawn to the ancient Alan settlements, tombs and underground crypts and the Christian churches dating from the tenth and eleventh centuries in the valleys and gullies of Zelenchuk and Mount Shoan.

Between Ossetia and Daghestan, along the Greater Caucasian Mountain Range, runs the land of the Vainakh – Republic of Chechnya. The word *vainakh* translates as "our people." This was the name by which the local highlanders distinguished themselves from the other inhabitants of the Caucasus. Many unique monuments of architecture — military and residential towers, sanctuaries, crypts and churches — were built between the River Terek and the basin of the River Argun in southern Chechnya, reflecting the

traditional way of life of the Vainakh. The laconic functionality and artistic expressiveness of the towers — the homes of the Vainakh people and original symbols of their land — are particularly outstanding.

Washed on the east by the Caspian Sea, Daghestan is the largest Caucasian republic in Russia. Traces of ancient civilisation have also been found here, including works from the Neolithic and Bronze Ages. The cave drawings and plastic art testify to the early assimilation of this region by man.

The Nogai steppe and the Trans-Caspian lowlands in the north, the feet and peaks of the Greater Caucasian Mountain Range and the rich and unique vegetation in the south define the natural diversity of Daghestan. Rare strains of beech, plane, oak and cornel grow here. The republic also abounds in minerals. The traditional arts and crafts of

Daghestan are world-famous — it is also celebrated for its embossed copper and carpets.

Daghestan is the third largest republic in the Russian Federation. It is also the most densely populated and multi-national in the Caucasus. It is difficult to find another place where, on such a comparatively small area, so many peoples speak so many different languages and follow so many different ways of life. Daghestan is traditionally known as the "mountain of languages." It is inhabited by 102 nationalities, belonging to three linguistic families — Nakho-Daghestanian, Indo-European and Turkic. The most numerous ethnic group in Daghestan is the Avars. The second largest is the Dargins, followed by the Kumyks, Lezghins, Laks, Tabasarans, Azeris, Chechens, Nogays, Tats, Rutuls, Aguls and Tsakhurs. Daghestan also has a Russian population, mostly Terek Cossacks inhabiting the lower reaches of the River Terek and its tributaries.

317

318

319

320

321

322

323

324

312. Greater Caucasian Mountain Range
313. Mountain summits
314, 318, 319, 322, 323. Caucasian Biosphere Reserve, Adygheya
315, 316, 324. In the environs of Guzeripl in Adygheya
317. Ceramicist at work in the village of Balkhar in Daghestan
320. Jug. 18th century. North Ossetia
321. On the road to Kubachi in Daghestan. The traditional arts and crafts of Daghestan are world-famous — artistic metal in Kubachi, ceramics in Balkar and wooden utensils, inlayed bone and mother-of-pearl in Untsukul.

325

326

327

328

329

It was in the 9th century AD that an integrated, early Russian state started forming in a long process of tribal unification that amalgamated into what became known as *Rus*. The capital of this early Russian kingdom was Kiev. The second most significant town, and the unofficial northern capital, was Novgorod. *Kievan Rus* did not last very long, splintering into warring sub-kingdoms in the 12th century. In the north, a politically and economically distinctive society developed. Known as the *Territory of Novgorod*, it was governed by a unique people's assembly, the *veche*, and occupied a vast expanse of flat land, forests, rivers and lakes. It was the largest territorial entity in Europe, extending from what is now Finland in the west to the Urals in the east, and from the Arctic Ocean in the north to Torzhok in the south. Novgorod is first mentioned in the chronicles as a settlement founded in 859 AD by the East Slavs. The name "Novgorod" means "New Town" and implies the existence of an earlier town, but historians have not been able to clarify

this. The city-state prospered through international trade; it was renowned for the acumen of its merchants and the quality of its craftsmen. But it also had enormous military-strategic significance, as became evident in the harrowing years of the 13th century. First, the Mongolian Khan Batu invaded Rus. While this cost the territory dearly in terms of plunder and war booty, Novgorod

325. Panoramic view of Novgorod, Kremlin and the Volkhov River
326. Liturgical vessel from St Sophia's
327, 328. At the Kremlin
329. The Kremlin. Bells of the 16th–17th centuries
330. The St Sophia Cathedral. 1045–50
331. St Sophia's Magdeburg (Sigtun) Gates. 12th century. Germany

330

331

In the centre of the Kremlin is an imposing bronze monument crowned with an orb and cross. This, one of the best-known sights of Novgorod, is called "The Millennium of Russia", designed by Mikhail Mikeshin. It was unveiled in 1862, a year after the abolition of serfdom and one thousand years after an event that marks the birth of Russia: the invitation of Rurik, leader of the Varangians, to Novgorod in 862. It stands 15.7 metres high, weighs 96 thousand tonnes, and has 129 bronze figures, 109 of them crafted in high relief on a rotunda base. The whole structure is divided into four sections, each displaying a different category of people who brought glory to Russia: princes and tsars, military figures and heroes, writers and artists, and clergy. Around the orb there are six fully sculpted figures, symbolizing six epochs in Russian history, from the summoning of the Varangians to the creation of the empire. The top of the monument is an Orthodox cross, held by an angel, and before it there is the figure of a woman kneeling. She personifies Russia.

332

333

334

335

remained as one of only two Russian towns (the other being Pskov) to escape total destruction at the hands of the invaders. Then Western crusaders tried to exploit the weakened state of Rus and subjected the region to menacing threats. Yet Novgorod prevailed, withstanding the pressure for a hundred years. By the 15th century the great principality of Muscovy (with its centre in Moscow) was becoming more and more influential. One by one, smaller feudal principalities started merging with Moscow to become part of a united Russian state. Novgorod, no longer the intimidating force it had once been, became a bone of contention between Moscow and the great principality of Lithuania.

From the 12th to 14th centuries Novgorod had been strong enough to repel any encroaching enemy. But internal rivalries

336

had weakened its strength and now, at a crucial moment in history, its warring factions were unable to unite. At the end of the 15th century, the great feudal republic collapsed. The bell of the people's assembly fell silent, the elected *posadniki* (governors) and *tysyatski* (high officials) disappeared, and Novgorod the Great became part of the united Russian state.

During the reign of Ivan the Fourth ("Ivan the Terrible"), the town was drawn into political turmoil rocking Muscovy in the form of the despotic terror known as the *oprichnina*. In 1570 the people of Novgorod were accused of "treason": it was alleged that they had again been plotting to switch their allegiance from Moscow to Lithuania. Ivan's special corps of *oprichniki* ransacked

332. The Kremlin. The Millennium of Russia Memorial. 1862

333. View of the Cathedral of St Nicholas-at-the-Court

334. Church of St Parasceva Piatnitsa-on-the-Marketplace. 1207

335, 336. View of Yaroslav's Court and the Marketplace

337. Icon: The Battle of the Suzdalians and the Novgorodians (The Miracle of the Icon Our Lady of the Sign).

338. Icon: St Nicholas. 1294

339. Icon: Sts Boris and Gleb. C. 1377.

340. Church of St Theodore Stratelates-on-the-Brook. 1360—61

341. Church of the Transfiguration on Ilyina Street. 1374

342. Cathedral of Our Lady of the Sign. 1682—88

343, 344. Zverin Convent of the Intercession (Founded in the 12th century)

The favourite building materials of local craftsmen were pine and fir; the timber of foliate species such as oak was not often used. Their favourite tools were the axe and the chisel. Novgorodians had long known about the saw (archaeological finds include 10th to 13th century hacksaws and frame-saws) but they used it in joinery only. All household items, ploughs, harrows, harnesses, furniture, crockery, and even the hut itself, were

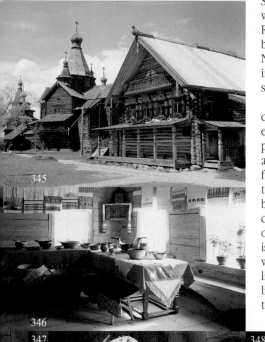

345

346

the town from 2 January until 13 February, taking priceless tributes with them when they left. At the beginning of the 16th century, during the so-called "Time of Troubles", Novgorod refused to recognize the protégé installed by False Dmitry's Polish troops and put up resistance to the foreign occupiers.

It was not until 1611 that Novgorod first ever submitted to foreign occupiers. The Swedes occupied the territory until 1617, wreaking havoc and ultimately cutting off Russian access to the Baltic Sea. This later became the prime reason for Peter the First's Northern Campaign, launched in 1700, during which Novgorod stood out as a major strategic point in the northwest.

The town then became a quiet provincial centre. It remained so until the first enemy bombs of the Second World War exploded in its streets. This occurred as early as July 1941; by August, after a lot of heavy fighting, Soviet troops had withdrawn from the town. For the next two and half years battles raged and there were thousands of casualties. The fallen soldiers are commemorated in obelisks and memorials. But there is also an eternal flame in memory of those who survived as well as those who died in liberating the town: it symbolizes ongoing life and willingness, among those who live, to remember those who died.

347

348

349

350 351

352

made entirely from natural materials. As they used to say in the old days: "the forest feeds wolf and man alike." People always strove to make their surroundings more decorative, more pleasant to live in. Peasant huts had carvings on gates, porch posts, roof cornices, lintels and frames. Everything that was required for everyday domestic life had to be pleasing to the eye. The museum workers at Vitoslavlitsy do more than just carefully preserve the early beginnings of our architec-

In 1964 work began on an open-air museum, to be called "Vitoslavlitsy". Wooden architecture has a rich tradition going back to the earliest days of Rus. Timber was the cheapest type of building material in this heavily forested area, and Novgorod the Great was built entirely by unknown local carpenters. But timber does not last, and it is only archaeological finds that give us any idea of what Novgorod looked like in that bygone era. Archaeologists have been working for over forty years to locate and preserve interesting structures in the Novgorod region. They often turn up in outlying villages and forests, where they cannot be looked after. For this reason, plans were drawn up in the 1960s for systematically identifying, removing and relocating these structures. Having them in one place makes appropriate conservation possible. The brilliant architect Leonid Krasnorechiev was the leading light behind this venture and now there are more than twenty interesting buildings standing in the open-air museum. At the beginning of each summer the Vitoslavlitsy Open-Air Museum hosts a folk festival. It is also an opportunity to hear old musical instruments, now all but forgotten.

tural heritage. They also make superb reproductions of traditional interiors, furnished with an assortment of the everyday items used by their peasant owners.

345, 346, 349–352. The Vitoslavlitsy Open-Air Museum of Wooden Architecture
347, 348, 353–355. Folklore festival at the museum
356. Church of the Annunciation from the village of Kuritsko. 1595
357. Windmill from the village of Ladoshchina. 1920s
358. Russian winter →

Alexander Sergeyevich Pushkin, the great Russian poet and prose writer, the founder of modern Russian literature and literary Russian, was born on 6 June 1799. The poet's father, Sergei Lvovich, belonged to an old family of the Russian nobility. After graduating from the Imperial Lyceum in Tsarskoe Selo, Alexander was employed at the Ministry of Foreign Affairs. In 1820, he was deliberately transferred to the south of Russia (Ekaterinoslav, Caucasus,

361

360

359

Crimea, Kishinev and Odessa). He was dismissed in 1824 and exiled to the village of Mikhailovskoe, where he was kept under police surveillance until 1826. Pushkin's novel in verse, Eugene Onegin, *is considered the greatest masterpiece of Russian literature. It has been a rich source of character types for Russian writers. Tatiana has been regarded as the ideal of Russian*

Besides Tsarskoe Selo, there was another place close to the heart of the great Russian poet Alexander Pushkin — the family estate of Mikhailovskoe in Pskov Province. "Haven of calm, labours and inspiration," Mikhailovskoe was a place where he could breathe freely, think, work and simply enjoy life. In 1742, Empress Elizabeth Petrovna awarded the lands of Mikhailovskoe in Pskov district to Major-General Ibrahim Hannibal,

"blackamoor of Peter the Great" and the poet's great-grandfather. These domains were inherited by his sons and grandsons. The small village of Mikhailovskoe became the property of Pushkin's mother.

The young poet came to Mikhailovskoe for the first time in 1817. A small manorhouse nestled among the surrounding fields and woods, the gentle blue waters of the River Sorot and the ruins of Voronich — an unas-

362

womanhood. The libretto for Tchaikovsky's opera was adapted from Pushkin's novel by the composer's brother Modeste. In the 1830s, Pushkin produced more prose than poetry. He married Natalia Goncharova in Moscow on 18 February 1831. The couple lived in St Petersburg, where they had a daughter Maria (1832), son Alexander (1833), son Grigory (1835) and daughter Natalia (1836). In the winter of 1837, the poet was insulted by Georges d'Anthès, a Frenchman adopted by the Dutch ambassador, Baron Heeckeren. Pushkin challenged D'Anthès to a duel. He was mortally wounded on 27 January, dying two days later.

359. Pushkin's house seen from the River Sorot at Mikhailovskoe
360. Pushkin's study. Detail
361. Mikhailovskoe country estate
362. Savkina Hill near Mikhailovskoe
363, 364. Vistas in Mikhailovskoe
365. Barn at Mikhailovskoe
366. Monument to Pushkin in the Pushkin Hills. 1959. Detail
367. Pushkin's grave in the Svyatogorsky Monastery
368. Steps leading to the Dormition Cathedral in the Svyatogorsky Monastery
369. Monastic bell-tower in the Pushkin Hills (Pushkinskiye Gory)

sailable fortress once guarding the Russian borders. Besides the manorhouse, the Mikhailovskoe estate also included a nanny's house and barns. An alley of fir trees leads to the Pushkin family chapel. This picturesque beauty spot includes Savkina Hill, where the poet enjoyed long walks. There he listened to legends and fairy tales told by his old nurse Arina Rodionovna, calling that process "making up for the defects in his accursed education" (meaning that his own tutors narrated him stories in French).

Sequestered in this secluded place, Pushkin found constant inspiration, allowing him to work with great focus. He wrote more than one hundred works, including four chapters of *Eugene Onegin*, *Boris Godunov*, *The Gypsies*, *Count Nulin* and dozens of poems, at Mikhailovskoe.

Pushkin's interest in Russian history brought him to the Dormition Monastery (Svyatogorsky). The abbey owned many books and manuscripts, which helped him during work on *Boris Godunov*. Pushkin observed the life of the brethren and conversed with the peasants visiting the boisterous monastic fairs, finding rich material for individual folk types and epic crowd scenes.

"*Pskov saved Russia from the greatest danger; the importance of this feat will live on in our memories for as long as we love our homeland and our names.*" *Russian historian Nikolai Karamzin wrote these words about the siege and heroic defence of Pskov in 1581—82. An enormous Polish-Lithuanian army led by King Stefan Batory attempted to first storm and then besiege the Pskov fortress — to no avail. No enemy ever managed to pass beyond Pskov.*

The high stone walls of the battlements are smooth and austere. Lined with deep and narrow arrow-holes, the unassailable turrets are positioned along the walls like sentries. The white-stoned town of Pskov stands on the Russian border, defending Kievan Rus, Muscovite Rus and the Russian Empire over the centuries.

378

379

380

381

382

The town of Pskov is first mentioned in the *Tale of Bygone Years* or *Russian Primary Chronicle* in 903, when Prince Igor of Kiev married a local woman called Olga. St Olga was famed for her political acumen. She helped to pave the way for the adoption of Christianity in Rus in 988, during the reign of her grandson, Prince Vladimir.

The Pskov Kremlin lies at the very heart of the historical town, occupying an elongated triangle at the junction of the Pskova and Velikaya rivers. Pskov was one of the largest towns in medieval Europe. The battlements were over six miles in length.

Although construction work was confined to the brief interludes between battles, this did not stop Pskov from developing into a handsome and well-structured town. The fortress walls, towers, monasteries, churches and the ground floors of houses were all built from stone.

378, 381, 382, 386. Kremlin. 11th to 17th centuries

379. Church of St Alexander Nevsky. 1906—08. Restored in 1995

380. Church of the Intercession and Nativity of the Virgin from Prolom. 17th century

383. Pogankin Chambers, 1620s—30s, one of the well-known examples of civil Pskov architecture. Now residence of Pskov State Museum of Art and History

384. Inner trap and tower of the Kremlin

385. Church of St Nicholas from Usokha. 1535

387. Cathedral of St John the Baptist in St John's Abbey. First half of the 17th century

388. Church of St Irene the Great Martyr. 15th century

389

390

389. Historical site of Toropets
390. Merchants' houses built
in Toropets in the 18th and
19th centuries
391. River Pererytitsa at Dostoyevsky's
house in Staraya Russa
Fedor Dostoyevsky briefly found
peace, quiet and the joy of family
life in the quiet provincial town
of Staraya Russa. In this modest
house drowning in the green of the
leafy willows growing on the banks
of the River Pererytitsa, the writer
worked on his immortal novel
The Brothers Karamazov.
392. Entrance to Fedor Dostoyevsky's
house
393. Fedor Dostoyevsky's study
394. Fedor Dostoyevsky's house
395. Porkhov fortress. 14th century

391

Staraya Russa, which now belongs to the Novgorod Province, is almost nine hundred years old. The famous Russian writer Fedor Dostoyevsky lived in the town for eight years. One of his novels, *The Brothers Karamazov*, is set in the town of Skotoprigonyevsk, which is based on Staraya Russa.

The small village of Izborsk is mentioned in the *Tale of Bygone Years* or *Russian Primary Chronicle*. In 862, when the legendary Varanghian princes were invited to Rus, Izborsk was ruled by Prince Truvor. The site of the historical settlement and cross of Truvor still survive. The original ancient settlement was not large, however, and, a new fortress was built on Crane Hill in the early fourteenth century. The fort was made of stone and had six battle turrets; the Germans called Izborsk an "iron town". In the fourteenth century, a cathedral was built in the fortress in honour of St Nicholas, patron saint of Izborsk.

Another fortress defended the approaches to Pskov on River Shelon, half-way between Lake Peipus and Lake Ilmen, where modern-day Porkhov now stands. It was founded in the thirteenth century by Prince Alexander Nevsky, who celebrated his wedding there.

In the seventeenth and eighteenth centuries, the inhabitants of Toropets were famed for their great skill in fishing for river pearls. The great Russian composer Modest

392

393 394

395

Mussorgsky was born in the surrounding area, which is now part of Tver Region.

Beginning as a fortress named *Oreshek* (or Nutlet) built by the Novgorod Republic in the source of the River Neva on Ladoga Lake, it had a key strategic position securing access to the Baltic Sea.

396, 399. Fortress on Crane Hill
in Izborsk. 14th and 15th centuries
397, 398. Izborsk landscapes
400. Trap in Izborsk fortress
401. How our ancestors fought on
the borders of the Pskov lands...
402. Oreshek fortress. Founded in 1323 →

FROM ST PETERSBURG
TO KALININGRAD

St Petersburg is the centre of the North-West Region of Russia. Its ideal geopolitical location offers unique transportation possibilities, with access to the Baltic, North, Norwegian and Barents Seas. This is of great political importance for Russia as the country's interests in Northern Europe have always been a priority. The Kaliningrad enclave on the Baltic Sea also plays an important role in Russia's co-operation with the Baltic States and countries in Northern Europe located near St Petersburg.

403

404

405

407

The city of St Petersburg, the former capital of the Russian Empire and the embodiment of the pride and glory of the Russian state, was founded on 27 May 1703. The creation of the city was a daring feat. For the first few years, construction work was centred on Hare Island. Here, the fortress of Sankt Pieter Burkh was erected as the nucleus of the future city. Its location was selected by Peter the Great himself who well understood the strategic advantages of placing such an outpost on the island in the Neva delta.

The fortress was designed as a closed rampart consisting of bastions and curtains (the part of the wall connecting the bastions). Peter was in a hurry to complete the job before the winter and so the construction of the fortifications was carried out under the supervision of the tsar's closest associates, thus the bastions are named in honour of these men, to wit, Naryshkin, Trubetskoy, Zotov, Golovkin and Menshikov. One of the southern bastions was built under the direct observation of Peter himself and consequently became known as the Tsar Bastion.

In order to get into the fortress it is necessary to cross the wooden St John's Bridge, pass through St John's Gate and then through a second gateway – St Peter's Gate. The triumphal arch of the latter still bears a beautifully preserved double-headed eagle (the coat-of-arms of the Russian Empire) wearing imperial crowns, made of lead and weighing over a tonne. A signal tower and flagpole for a special fortress standard, were installed on the Naryshkin Bastion, which also became the site of a cannon, fired every day at noon, a tradition that has been preserved to this day.

The main building within the fortress is the Sts Peter and Paul Cathedral – the imperial burial-vault. Its belfry together with the gilded spire and figure of an angel, the guardian of the city, stands at a height of 122.5 metres. The figure of the angel serves as a weather vane. In 1992, a statue of Peter I was erected on the square in front of the guardhouse and soon became the subject of

great debate. This unusual image is quite different to the typical representations of the tsar-creator and tsar-victor that prevailed in the monumental sculptures of centuries gone by. Yet the longer the statue "lives" in the fortress, the more normal its presence becomes. The Peter and Paul Fortress never served a direct military purpose, since no enemy ever made it as far as its walls. Very soon after it had been built, however, it began to be used as a political prison and torture-chamber. Over the course of two hundred years, its bastions and casemates held countless state prisoners.

403. Peter and Paul Fortress.
   View of Cathedral Square. Sts Peter and Paul Cathedral. 1712–33.
   Architect Domenico Trezzini.
   Boat House. 1762–65
404. Detail of St Peter's Gate.
   The "state eagle" of Russia
405. White Nights. The fortress through the Palace Bridge opening
406. St John's Gate
407. Signal guns on the Naryshkin Bastion
408. Interior of the cathedral
409. Statue of Peter I. 1992. Sculptor Mikhail Shemiakin

408

409

410

After it had been decreed in 1712 that the imperial court was to move from Moscow to the banks of the Neva, the northern city began to be developed in accordance with a plan that had been drawn up previously by local and foreign experts. Vasilievsky Island was originally intended to become the heart of the emerging city. Peter was particularly fond of Amsterdam and hoped that the new capital would somehow remind him of that place.

410, 414. Rostral Columns. 1805–10

411. Panoramic view of the Neva and Vasilievsky Island

412. Stock Exchange (Naval Museum). 1805–16. Architect Jean-François Thomas de Thomon

413. View of the University Embankment. Kunstkammer (now, Peter the Great Anthropological and Ethnological Museum). 1718–34. Architects Georg Mattarnovi, Gaetano Chiaveri and Mikhail Zemtsov

411

412

413

414

For a hundred years Vasilievsky Island was the site of the city's port. At the beginning of the 19th century, it was moved further downstream, and now only the wrought iron rings set in the granite walls of the embankment serve as a reminder of the fact that ships once moored here. The spit of Vasilievsky Island was designed to reflect Petersburg's status as an international centre of shipping and commerce. The centrepiece of the resulting architectural composition is the Stock Exchange, which resembles a Doric-style temple. The main façade, overlooking the Neva, is adorned with the figures of the sea god Neptune and his retinue, while on the western side an allegorical embodiment of Navigation stands alongside the god of commerce, Mercury. Although Mercury is no longer worshipped here, the building remains faithful to the fierce god of the sea: today, the Stock Exchange is the home of the Naval Museum.

It was planned to create a network of streets and canals, which would drain the marshy land, on Vasilievsky Island. Although this project was not brought to completion, the right-angled arrangement of the streets and the three main avenues which form the architectural basis of the area today almost coincides with the initial plan. The so-called Bolshoy (Large), Sredny (Medium), and Maly (Small) Prospekts run from west to east and are intersected from north to south by 34 "lines", which open out onto the Neva.

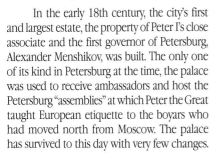

In the early 18th century, the city's first and largest estate, the property of Peter I's close associate and the first governor of Petersburg, Alexander Menshikov, was built. The only one of its kind in Petersburg at the time, the palace was used to receive ambassadors and host the Petersburg "assemblies" at which Peter the Great taught European etiquette to the boyars who had moved north from Moscow. The palace has survived to this day with very few changes.

Downstream from the Lieutenant Schmidt Bridge, freight ships, tankers and tourist liners from far and wide line the banks of Vasilievsky Island and the English Embankment. On very rare occasions, when Petersburg happens to be one of the finishing points of the international Cutty Sark Tall Ships' Races, the river becomes crowded with sailboats and the façades of the elegant residences lining the banks are obscured by a forest of masts and rigging.

415. Menshikov Palace. 1710s. Architects Giovanni Mario Fontana, Gottfried Johann Schaedel
416. Building of the Twelve Collegia (now the University). 1722–42. Architect Domenico Trezzini
417. University Embankment. Pier in front of the Academy of Arts. 1832–34. Architect Konstantin Thon Sphinx (Egypt, 13th century B.C.)
418. Lieutenant Schmidt Embankment Statue of Admiral Krusenstern 1873. Sculptor Ivan Schroeder
419. Academy of Arts. 1764–88. Architects Jean-Baptiste Vallin de La Mothe, Alexander Kokorinov
420. View of the English Embankment from the Bridge
421. Pribaltiyskaya Hotel. 1972–78. Architect N. Baranov

422. Monument to Peter the Great
(The Bronze Horseman).
1782. Sculptor Etienne-Maurice
Falconet

423. Senate and Synod. 1829—36.
Architect Carlo Rossi

424. Decembrists Square (formerly
Senate Square)

425. Two riders

426. Admiralty Embankment (Palace
Pier). Statue of Peter the Carpenter.
1880. Sculptor Leopold Bernstam

In 1704, on Admiralty Island, situated on the left bank of the Neva and bordered to the south by the Moika, work began on the building of a shipyard that was designed by Peter the Great himself. Together with the Peter and Paul Fortress, the Admiralty Shipyard became one of the city's main architectural features. In the 1730s, the architect Ivan Korobov abandoned the original plans

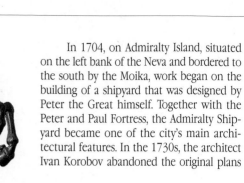

422

423

424

425

426

for the Admiralty and replaced the frame-built warehouses with stone buildings. Moreover, he masterminded the construction of a tower with a tall gilded spire (now, 72 m high) topped with a weather vane in the shape of a three-sailed frigate. At the beginning of the 19th century, the Admiralty underwent fundamental reconstruction under the watchful eye of Andrean Zakharov. The Neo-Classical architect, while preserving Korobov's original concept, considerably enlarged the building and enhanced its appearance using sculptural designs. The New Admiralty was envisaged as a unique monument to the Russian fleet, thus its main entrance was given the form of a triumphal arch. Zakharov repeated the motif of the wide archway in the façades of the two symmetrically placed pavilions that face the Neva. The sculptural embellishments that indicate the purpose served by the Admiralty play an important part in the composition of the building as a whole. The idea of the synthesis of architecture and sculpture was central to Neo-Classical design and

427 428

was first clearly demonstrated in Zakharov's work. He presented sculpture in all its manifestations, from freestanding statues to sculpted ornament, united by a single theme – the glorification of Russia's naval prowess.

In the late 18th century, Decembrists Square was known as Peter's Square because of the monument to Peter I (the first equestrian statue in Petersburg) that was erected there in 1782. The Senate, the Synod and the Admiralty serve as the striking wings to a stage upon which the main player is the Emperor – Peter the Great. The French sculptor Etienne Falconet's most immaculate work of art was immortalised by the great Russian poet, Alexander Pushkin, in "The Bronze Horseman". Falconet's monument to Peter the Great is the centrepiece of Decembrists Square, and its striking outline is clearly visible even from afar. The monument is a sculptural symbol of an entire

epoch of Russian history. It fuses the energy and many aspects of the Emperor – Creator, Reformer and Lawmaker – into one.

Peter's Square became known as Senate Square in the early 19th century due to the construction of the majestic edifice of the Senate and the Synod (1829–36).

Senate Square was rechristened in honour of a key event in the history of Russia in 1925 (to commemorate its 100th anniversary). On 14 December 1825, the ranks of demonstrators in the first organised protest for freedom, the Constitution and human rights lined up at the foot of the "Bronze Horseman". The insurgent regiments were gunned down and the uprising suppressed. The five leaders were subsequently executed and the remaining protesters permanently exiled to Siberia. The forms and symbols of Senate Square have become part of both the history and legend of Petersburg.

429

On the attic of the Admiralty tower, The Establishment of a Fleet in Russia *is depicted in high relief. Covering a length of 22 metres, this frieze plays an important visual and symbolic role in the decor of the building. Statues of ancient mythological and historical characters look down from the four corners of the parapet of the Admiralty tower. In front of the main entrance, on either side of the triumphal arch, stand the monumental figures of three sea nymphs holding orbs. Mounted on high pedestals, they are supposed to symbolise the free passage of the Russian fleet across the globe.*

427. Caravel at the top of the Admiralty spire serves as a weathervane.
428. Admiralty Embankment. Eastern pavilion of the Admiralty
429. Admiralty. 1806–19. Architect Andrean Zakharov
430. The attic of the Admiralty tower with the relief *The Establishment of a Fleet in Russia*
431. Figures of sea nymphs

430 431

Between 1856 and 1859, under the supervision of the architect Montferrand a monument was erected to Nicholas I in the centre of St Isaac's Square. The model of the equestrian statue itself was made by Piotr von Klodt, who personally participated in the casting of it. The sculptor's precise mathematical calculations made it possible to use just two points of support in the mounting of the horse. The resulting sculptural group creates a striking effect when viewed from any point on the square or the neighbouring streets. The masterful execution of the central statue together with the monument's fortuitous location make it a work of genuine artistic value. The artists Ramazanov and

432

433

Salemann took part in the creation of the sculpture. These allegorical characters, which resemble Nicholas I's wife and daughters, symbolise the Christian virtues: Faith (with the cross and the Gospels), Wisdom (holding a mirror), Justice (bearing the scales), and Might (with a lance and shield).

434

435

St Isaac's Cathedral was intended to be the greatest in the Russian Empire. Vast amounts of money and effort were required to construct this building, which stands at a height of 101.5 metres and covers over a hectare of land. It is the fourth largest domed cathedral of its type in the world after St Peter's in Rome, St Paul's in London and Santa Maria dei Fiori in Florence. The building that is to be seen today – the fourth to bear the name of St Isaac's – was built over the course of 40 years in accordance with designs by the architect Auguste Montferrand. Rectangular in shape, the body of the building has four columned porticoes, which make the vast bulk appear even larger than it already is. The interior of the cathedral (4,000 sq.m.) boasts a profusion of murals and mosaics. The best painters and sculptors of the time contributed to this unusual work of art. Central to the interior decor of St Isaac's Cathedral is the combination of coloured marbles, malachite, lapis and gilt, which creates a sumptuous setting for the many magnificent sculptures, paintings and mosaics. Due to the difficulty of maintaining a steady temperature within the building, it was originally planned to replace the initial paintings with mosaics.

432. St Isaac's Cathedral. 1818–58. Architect Auguste Montferrand
433. Statues decorating the outer colonnade of the dome
434. Figures of angels around a lamp
435, 436. St Isaac's central dome and central nave
437. Iconostasis. Mosaic: St Nicholas. 1855–62. Designed by Timofei Neff
438. St Isaac's chancel
439. St Isaac's Square. Monument to Nicholas I. 1856–59. Mariinsky Palace. 1839–44
440, 441. Interiors of the Mariinsky Palace

442. Panorama of Palace Square
443. Winter Palace. Main Staircase
(Jordan Staircase). 1754—62.
Architect Bartolomeo Rastrelli;
1838—39. Architect Vasily Stasov
444. Winter Palace. Boudoir. 1850s —
1860s. Architect Harald Bosse
445. Gold comb: Fighting Scythians.
4th century B.C. Solokha
burial mound.
Plaque in the shape of a deer.
Late 7th — early 6th century B.C.
Barrow near Kostromskaya,
Northern Caucasus

442

443

444

Palace Square did not gain its current title until the middle of the 18th century when the Winter Palace, the home of the Russian Emperors from 1763 to 1917, was erected along the northern edge overlooking the Neva. Today, the Winter Palace is one of five buildings that make up the architectural ensemble of the State Hermitage Museum. It is generally believed that the Hermitage was established as a museum in 1764, when Catherine II purchased a collection belonging to the merchant Johann Gotzkowsky, which included 225 canvases by renowned Western European masters. Today, the Hermitage collection, which has been put together over the course of more than two centuries, numbers about three million exhibits. Although the Hermitage's collection of Italian paintings does not span every period of the country's rich artistic history, it is able to compete with some of the world's most famous Italian collections by virtue of the quality of the works on dis-

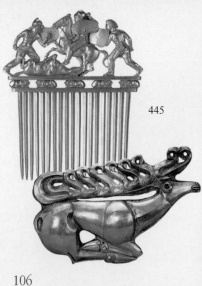

445

446

447

play and the renown of the men who created them. Without a doubt, two of the most outstanding and famous works to be seen here are the canvases known as *The Madonna Benois* and *The Madonna Litta*, painted by Leonardo da Vinci. The Hermitage's collection of Dutch and Flemish art ranks amongst the greatest in the world in terms of breadth and quality. The greatest of the Dutch masters, Rembrandt, is represented by 25 of his paintings, including *Flora*, *Danae* and *The Return of the Prodigal Son*. The achievements

and life-affirming nature of Flemish art, which is characterised by an extensive palette and an acute sense of form and movement, are essentially summed up in the works of the leading artist of this particular school, Rubens. The Hermitage's collection of Impressionism, Post-Impressionism, Fauvism and Cubism is famed throughout the world. Of particular interest are the articles of Scythian culture, found during the excavation of burial mounds in the valley of the River Kuban.

446. New Hermitage. Small Skylight Room. 1842–51. Architect Leo von Klenze
447. Winter Palace. Peter the Great Hall. 1833. Architect Auguste Montferrand; 1842. Architect Vasily Stasov
448. *Venus of Tauride*. Roman copy from the original of 3rd century B.C.
449. Giorgione (Giorgio da Castelfranco). 1478(?)–1510. *Judith*. 1500s
450. Pierre-Auguste Renoir. 1841–1919 *Girl with a Fan*. 1881
451. Henri Matisse. 1869–1954 *Dance*. 1910

452. Pablo Picasso. 1881–1973 *Woman with a Fan (After the Ball)*. 1908
453. Leonardo da Vinci. *The Madonna Litta*. 1490
454. Peter Paul Rubens. 1577–1640 *The Union of Earth and Water*. C. 1618
455. Rembrandt Harmensz. van Rijn. 1606–1669 *The Return of the Prodigal Son*. 1668–1669
456. New Hermitage. Hall of Twenty Columns. 1842–51. Architect Leo von Klenze
457. New Hermitage. Portico with Atlases. 1848. Architect Leo von Klenze. Sculptor Alexander Terebenev

No description of St Petersburg would be complete without some mention of the former imperial residences that are strung out around the edges of the northern capital like the beads of an exquisite necklace. Many of these park and palace complexes came into being at the same time as the city and, in accordance with Peter I's plans, became a delightful and fitting frame for Petersburg.

Tsarskoe Selo is associated primarily with the names of two Empresses, Elizabeth Petrovna and Catherine the Great. During the reign of Elizabeth and through the efforts of Francesco Bartolomeo Rastrelli, who believed that palaces should be created "for the common glory of Russia", that this residence could rightfully be called Tsarskoe Selo – the Tsar's Village. One of the main features of the palace was, without a doubt, the famous Amber Room. In 1717, amber panels were sent as a gift to Peter I by the Prussian king, Frederick I. On 31 May 2003, the jubilee of St Petersburg, the ceremony of the inauguration of the Amber Room destroyed in World War II was held.

498, 499. Tsarskoe Selo. Catherine Palace. 1752–56. Architect Bartolomeo Rastrelli. Sculptor Johann Dunker

500, 501. Catherine Palace. Interiors

502. Catherine Park. Hermitage Pavilion. 1749–54. Architect Bartolomeo Francesco Rastrelli

503. View of the Agate Rooms and Catherine Palace

504. Cameron Gallery. 1784–87. Architect Charles Cameron

505. Peterhof. Grand Cascade. Decorative sculpture

506. Monplaisir Palace and Monplaisir Garden. 1714–23. Architects Johann Braunstein, Jean-Baptiste Leblond, Niccolo Michetti. Sculptor Carlo Rastrelli Designed by Peter I

507. Grand Cascade. Fountain: Samson Tearing Open the Jaws of the Lion. 1801. Sculptor Mikhail

Kozlovsky. Architect Andrei
Voronikhin; cast by V. Ekimov
508. View of the Grand Canal
509. Panorama of the Great Palace
and Grand Cascade
510. Statue of Poseidon and panorama
of the Marly Palace
511. Gulf of Finland →

Peterhof, the favourite residence of Peter I, after whom it is named, constitutes a grandiose 18th–19th century architectural and park ensemble with an area of over a thousand hectares dotted with approximately thirty buildings and pavilions and decorated with over one hundred sculptures. The arrangement of fountains on the terraces and in the lower park was developed and a gravity-fed water system installed in the Petrine era. By skilfully exploiting the lay of the extensive territory with its natural ledges, slopes and plains, architects, engineers and sculptors succeeded in creating a picturesque park and peerless architectural ensemble. In front of the northern façade of the palace, stretching down towards the sea, is the Lower Park, which embraces a variety of buildings and numerous fountains. At the centre of this magnificent symmetrical composition is the Grand Cascade.

KALININGRAD

The Kaliningrad Oblast is known as the Amber Region — ninety percent of the world's "sun stone" reserves are located here. The flora and fauna of this Baltic Sea territory are varied and unique, the region being famed for its exceptional, distinctive beauty. Of particular note is the Curonian Sandbar — a narrow sandy peninsula in the Baltic Sea with a long ridge of amazingly white dunes.

512. Solnechnogorsk. The beach
513. The Kaliningrad Sea Trade Port
514. The Kaliningrad Amber Museum. Located in the Dohna Tower

The victory of countries in the anti-Hitler coalition during the Second World War changed the map of Europe. The USSR, whose people forged this victory while suffering great losses and making tremendous sacrifices, acquired the territory of East Prussia. The most westerly point in today's Russia is the Kaliningrad Oblast, an enclave on the Baltic Sea. Washed by the waters of the Baltic, this ancient region has a unique history and destiny. Its centre, as in the former age of East Prussia, is the city of Kaliningrad, previously known by its German name of Königsberg. Of immense strategic significance, Königsberg also enjoyed the status of a capital city and citadel. A member of the Hanseatic League, it was already involved in trade with Old Russia, primarily with Novgorod the Great. In the 17th and 18th centuries it was one of the

517

516

(1858, designed by Montalembert),
formerly part of Königsberg's
internal defences
515. The Curonian Sandbar.
Sand dunes
516. Svetlogorsk. The town park.
Girl with Jug. 1940.
Sculptor Hermann Brachert
517. Kaliningrad. Cathedral.
Founded in 1297
518. Zelenogradsk
519. Svetlogorsk. The water-tower
of the warm seawater clinic.
1908
520. Baltiisk. The Amber Shore
521. Sunset on the Baltic

largest Baltic Sea ports and was famed for
its university. E. T. A. Hoffmann and Imman-
uel Kant were both born in Königsberg.
It was here that the great philosopher gave
lectures, and it was here that he found his
final resting-place.

The region has retained its unique history and architecture. Remnants of fortresses, such as towers, bastions, gateways, rave-
lins and forts as well as churches and public
buildings dating from the 14th to the 19th centuries bear witness to the former glory of

Kaliningrad (Königsberg). There are many
historic areas in the region of importance
in Russian and European history, such as
Sovetsk, Baltiisk, Bagrationovsk and Svetlogorsk (formerly known as Tilsit, Pillau,
Preußisch Eyla and Rauschen respectively).

529. Bolshoi Solovetsky Island. View
from the Holy Lake onto the
Transfiguration of the Saviour
Monastery (founded 1430s)
530. St Nicholas's Church. 1831–33
531. St Nicholas and Korozhnaya
Towers, 16th century

529

530

531

532

533

534

In a letter to a friend, the outstanding Russian artist Mikhail Nesterov wrote "Go to Solovki, you will be closer to God". And, in truth, for almost six centuries the bleak Northern cloister on the Solovki Islands of the White Sea has been a true phenomenon in the eyes of the world, created by its inhabitants, hermits and, at times, convicts, all in the name of love, goodness and the triumph of spirit.

The Solovki Monastery was founded by Fathers Herman and Sabbatius, who arrived in this barren region in 1429. One year after Sabbatius's death the hermit Zosima came to Solovki. In 1548–1566 under the monastery's Father Superior Philip, stone churches appeared and the archipelago began to be cultivated. The Solovki Monastery thus became not just one of the most important in Russia, but the true heart of the White Sea region – politically, economically and spiritually. Fish-ponds were established on the island, a lake and canal system constructed to provide drinking water, brick and pottery factories built and reindeer breeding begun. By the late 16th century the main settlement was surrounded by mighty stone walls with eight towers – the monks had to repel Swedish invasions several times. The monastery was also beautified with the stone Church of the Transfiguration, the Church of the Annunciation and the Church of the Dormition. The preserved relics of Father Sabbatius were immured behind the altar of the latter in 1465. There were also plans to build a huge five-hundred meter refectory close to the cathedral. The complex was immense, including a further six smaller monasteries and three hermitages! The oldest is the Sabbatius Monastery, which originally housed the icons of Sabbatius and Herman. It is located two kilometres from Sekirnaya Hill, one of the highest points on Solovki. The monasteries and hermitages blend naturally into the landscape, creating a particular feel of harmony of the human spirit and nature. But it was not just prayers and seclusion that "defined the features" of the monastery. Salt, hunting, the sea, mica, pearls and other trades allowed this amazing stronghold of the Russian State, lost in cold, Northern waters close to the Arctic Circle, to exist and develop. There are many bitter pages in the history of the Solovki Islands. Events of the 20th century proved particularly tragic. The Solovki Monastery became a veritable "Calvary" for many great Russian people in the 1920s–30s. The wretchedly notorious Solovki Special Purpose Camp (SLON), where thousands of political prisoners were tortured, was established in despoiled churches. During the Great Patriotic War, Solovki was

home to the Training Unit of the Northern Fleet and the Solovki Sea Cadets' School, graduates of which served on every single one of the nation's fleets. In the 1980s work began to restore the architectural ensemble, and in 1992 the monastery's spiritual life was reborn.

Carving from the North of Russia was an ancient and unique artistic craft, alongside the difficult work of hunting and fishing, and it was linked to everyday life. Craftsmen used lathes to work the bones of walruses, mammoths and domesticated animals, as well as employing techniques of whittling,

532, 533. Refectory. Gallery and porch
534. Annunciation Church
   (16th century), Abbot's Wing
   (19th century) and Gulf
   of Prosperity
535, 536. Sea dyke. 19th century
537. Drying a kelp on Bolshoi
   Solovetsky Island
538, 539. Studfarm on Bolshoi
   Solovetsky Island.
   Bitterly cold are winters here with
   strong icy winds and much snow,
   autumns are astonishingly
   colourful.

The life of a peasant in this region was very hard. He earned his living mainly from fishing. The climate is so cold that cabbages, onions, buckwheat and oats which used to be the main foodstuff for the Russians don't grow here. Lands are swampy and covered with endless forests, that's why a cart, a traditional vehicle of peasants, could not run there. Even in summer local people used sledges pulled by horses or simply rode horses. During long northern winters when it grew dark early peasants told legends and sang byliny *(narrative poetry). Bitterly cold are winters here with strong icy winds and much snow, autumns are astonishingly colourful.*

540

541

engraving and colouring. Jewellery, icons, portraits and household items are now on display in many museums both in Russia and abroad in addition to being used as everyday objects.

Russia's North is a region of wild nature, a region of courageous people – hunters and fishermen, lumber-men, carpenters and shipbuilders. In a constant struggle with encroaching nature, in labour, in feats of arms, in devout religious convictions, this is where the freedom-loving, integral and independent characteristics of the Russian people were forged.

The opening up of the Northern territories is linked to the period when Russian Statehood and Russian culture began to

542 543 544 545 546

547
548
549

emerge. It is in the North of Russia that the best examples of folk art and folklore have remained in their purest, original form. The wooden buildings in this region form one of the finest examples of architecture in Russia. Here creative toil can be seen in the beautiful buildings generally constructed by unknown craftsmen, who raised majestic cathedrals and modest chapels, vast peasant country estates and intricate windmills and wells. A study of wooden architecture in Northern Russia explains the "history of the abandonment of wooden forms in favour of stone constructions" (Igor Grabar) that defined the nature and principles of Russian architecture as a whole.

Founded in 1584 on the decree of Ivan the Terrible at the mouth of the Northern Dvina, Arkhangelsk is the major city in the region. Initially, the city emerged as the Russian State's naval centre. As a result, it was the first Russian port connecting Russia with Western Europe. The city developed further under Peter I, who built a wharf, an admiralty and a fortress.

Not far from Arkhangelsk lies the famous village of Kholmogory. It was famed from the 12th century as a major trading point for Novgorod the Great. For five cen-

turies now, bone carvers have worked here, passing their craft from one generation to the next. Kholmogory is the birthplace of Mikhail Lomonosov. There is a memorial site dedicated to the great scientist's life.

The North of Russia stretches to the Barents Sea. The Kolsky peninsula and adjacent mainland made up the "Murman" territory, with people coming from Novgorod even in ancient times. Today, the Murmansk Region – a nature reserve area with the Khibin Mountans, tundra, forest-tundra and taiga forests – draws myriad tourists throughout the year. The region's centre is the city of Murmansk, an ice-free Russian port which was named Romanov-na-Murman when it was founded in 1916.

540. St Nicholas's Church in Kovda village in Murmansk Region. 1651
541. Lyavlya village in Arkhangelsk Region
542, 543, 545, 546. Malye Karely, Museum of Wooden Architecture and Folk Art, Arkhangelsk
544. A warm welcome
547. Kondopoga Region near Lake Onega
548. Lake Onega
549. Murmansk commercial port
550. Monument to Peter the Great in Arkhangelsk. 1911. Sculptor Marcus Antokolsky
551. Arkhangelsk seen from the North Dvina
552. Arkhangelsk. Ice Composition. 2004
553. Northern motif →

550
551
552

The town of Totma is famous for its churches of unusual proportions. Their massive volumes contrast with the elegant, upward aspiring tops. The decor of the churches is unusual; the plastic ornamentation decorating the walls recalls the vignettes and cartouches on old maps. Perhaps this is why the town produced so many famous explorers and travellers, including the discoverer of "Russian America". There are many museums in Totma, including

577

578

579

580

Vologda is almost the same age as Moscow. Like many other large Russian towns, its chronicles abound with tales of events of national importance. Vologda's geographical position meant that it was often drawn into the internecine warfare waged during the formation of the Russian state. Ivan the Terrible often visited the town and even planned to make it the capital of his kingdom. The architectural ensembles of the kremlin or citadel were built in the sixteenth century. The most important administrative and church buildings were concentrated here. The foundations of the majestic five-cupola cathedral were laid in 1568. The cathedral took two and a half years to build. Its forms and appearance recall the most important place of worship in Russia — the Dormition Cathedral in the Moscow Kremlin. In the late seventeenth century, the walls of the cathedral were decorated with brightly patterned frescoes painted by masters from Yaroslavl. The Archbishop's Yard was designed as the official residence of the bishop of Vologda and Perm, a post re-established by Ivan the Terrible. The Chambers of Bishop Joseph II, built almost two centuries later, rank among the finest examples of Russian Baroque architecture from the reign of Empress Elizabeth (1741—61). The chambers are now a museum complex and home to a priceless collection of historical relics and Old Russian and

581

folk art. One mile outside Vologda lies the Prilutsky Monastery of the Saviour. Founded by St Dmitry of Priluki in 1371, the abbey was one of the most important spiritual centres and military outposts in northern Russia. St Dmitry of Priluki was a leading Russian churchman and scholar from the town of Pereyaslavl-Zalessky who followed the teachings of St Sergius of Radonezh.

According to official documents, Veliky Ustyug is only sixty years younger than

the Museum of Russian Church History, Museum of Seamen and the memorial museum of the famous explorer Ivan Kuskov. The town is also celebrated for its salt mines and historical salt furnaces.

576. Cupolas of St Sophia Cathedral
577—580. Vologda Kremlin
(founded in 1565)
581. Saviour of Prilutsky Monastery
(founded in 1371)
582—584. Veliky Ustyug — home
of Father Christmas
585. Trinity Cathedral in Veliky
Ustyug. 1559 — late 17th century
586. Church of the Entry into Jerusalem
in Totma. 1774—94
587. Church of the Presentation
in Solvychegodsk. 1609—93
588—590. North Russian landscapes

Moscow. The "town" of Ustyug is mentioned in the early Russian chronicles. Later, during the reign of Ivan the Terrible, it was awarded the appendage of Veliky or "Great", an honour given to few Russian towns. Veliky Ustyug occupies an exceptional geographical position, stretched out along the bank of the River Sukhona, which merges with the River Yug near the town to form the North Dvina. Standing on a major trade route and waterway, Ustyug was an important centre of commerce and crafts. Politically, even in the early period of its history, it gravitated towards Moscow. The main face of Veliky Ustyug is the numerous churches, bell towers, trading arcades and historical mansions lining the embankment of the River Sukhona. The town is famous for its traditional arts and crafts, including niello on silver, enamel, filigree and wood and bark carvings. The northern frosts and snows and the special air of creativity, spiritual harmony and time-honoured folk traditions make Veliky Ustyug the natural centre of Yuletide festivities in Russia and the traditional home of Father Christmas.

591

592

The Urals is the only chain of mountains diving Europe from Asia, separating the East European and West Siberian Plains. The Ural Mountains stretch for over two thousand kilometres from north to south. Their width ranges from forty to 150 kilometres. The highest peak is Mount Narodnaya. The territory is closely connected to the regions lying before, near and beyond the Ural Mountains. The area has been divided by geographers into the Arctic, Subarctic, North, Middle and South Urals. The Asian part of Russia, right up to the Pacific Ocean, is known as Siberia. Looking from Europe, the Urals are the starting point of Siberia. From the point of view of China or Japan, however, Siberia does not begin, but ends at the Urals.

Stretching for hundred and hundreds of miles, this great mountain range has been known for thousands of years. The Greeks called the Urals the Riphean mountains, correctly guessing that the rivers and streams flowing in these hills contained gold, while the soil contained countless riches. Although they abounded in animals, birds and fish, the mountains themselves were inaccessible, hidden behind primeval forests and inaccessible cliffs. On a map accompanying Ptolemy's *Geographia*, published in Rome in 1490, the Urals are called the Hyperborea Mountains. Before the eighteenth century, the name "Urals" did not figure on a single map. The mountains were called the Stone Belt (or simply Stones), while the River Ural was called the Yaikà. The Ural Mountains owes its current name to the famous Russian ethnographer and statesman Vasily Tatischev. The River Yaikà was renamed the River Ural by Catherine the Great as a punishment, following the participation of the Yaika Cossacks in the Pugachev rebellion of 1773.

The austere mountainous country on the border between Europe and Asia – "casket of countless natural riches" – provided the inspiration for many remarkable myths.

591. Arctic Ural. Maldy-Nyrd Mountain Chain
592. Statuette made from cast iron of Kasli, Cheliabinsk Province
593. The South Urals. River Belaya
594. The South Urals. River Aya
595. The Middle Urals. River Chusovaya
596. Bounty of nature
597. Izba shutters

POLAR REGION, SIBERIA, FAR EAST

Despite the differences in their natural, climatic and social conditions, the historical territory of Siberia includes the lands beyond the Arctic Circle, Altai, Baikal and the Far East. The largest region of Russia covers a landmass greater than Canada, the second largest country in the world. The fantastic wealth of the natural resources of these territories proves that Mikhail Lomonosov was right when he predicted, back in the eighteenth century, that the wealth of Russia would be doubled by Siberia.

POLAR REGION

The Arctic is part of the Far North. The name comes from the Greek word *arktos*, which the Ancient Greeks used to describe the constellation of the Great Bear, which always shone to the north of Hellas. The Arctic is now the term for the northern polar region of the globe adjoining the North Pole. This region extends as far as the Arctic Circle, inside which the sun does not set at all on 21 June. The Russian section of the Arctic contains five seas and the northern part of the Bering Sea.

One famous feature of the northern winter nights is the Aurora Borealis or Northern Lights. A pale green shroud spreads across the sky, while iridescent streams of

The Taimyr peninsular is the northernmost territory of the Asian landmass. Located between the Arctic Circle and the North Pole, it is washed by the Kara and Laptev Seas. The blanket of snow lies for three hundred days of the year. In December in Taimyr, the daylight only lasts from noon to two o'clock and is indiscernible during a blizzard. When the snowstorm abates, the frost hardens. Fifty degrees below zero is no rarity. The long-awaited first herald of the sun comes in February. Fedor Dostoyevsky was right when he wrote: "What one ray of sunshine can do to a man's soul!" The price of this ray of sunshine is extremely high in the Arctic Circle after a long polar night. In May, the sun does not disappear beyond the horizon for days on end. The earth does not throw off its shroud of snow until the middle of June, when it is adorned with bright flowers. In the light summer days and nights,

a strange and unearthly light transform into a bright, crimson glow. The effect is reminiscent of an enormous fan of multi-coloured feathers of a firebird. Shimmering, folding and unfolding, they break out into pink and green flames.

The polar bear was always particularly revered among the people of the Far North. The Nenets people considered the face or paw of this animal the "firmest oath". Special rules govern the consumption of their meat. Women, for example, do not eat it. For its strength, agility and quick mind, the Chukcha people call the polar bear the umka *(from the Russian word* um *for "mind"). Prohibitions on the shooting*

628

629

630

631

when the beauty of the tundra and forest-tundra is particularly unique, one understands their magnetic attraction to anyone who has seen them at least once. Traces of the mammoth and the musk-ox have been excavated in Taimyr.

In 2000, the world's only museum of the musk-ox and mammoth opened in the town of Khatanga. Dozens of sporting expeditions pass through Khatanga, travelling on skies along the drifting ice floes or by helicopter towards the North Pole.

On the right bank of the River Yenisei is Dudinka – the administrative centre of Taimyr district and the northernmost town on earth. One of the five northernmost towns in the world – Norilsk – lies amid the empty tundra expanses of this hostile peninsula, two degrees north of the Arctic Circle. The Norilsk Mountains are rich in copper-nickel ores and high-quality coal. The construction

632

of polar bears have led to an increase in their numbers. The polar bear symbolises the bio-equilibrium of the Arctic, directly reflecting the state of the environment of the Arctic Ocean. The animal immediately reacts to pollution of the water with oil, fleeing from the polluted zone, where the plankton die, leading to the disappearance of fish and, as a result, seals.

621. Arctic Circle obelisk in Salekhard
622. Will it never be spring again?
623. Cape Dezhneva in the Bering Strait
624. Snow-clearing machine
625. Guide to Vorkuta prisons (ex-GULAGs)
626, 628, 630, 632. Constructing the Transsiberian Gas Pipeline
627. 67th parallel in Vorkuta
629. Oil well in Yamal
631. Oil rig in the River Lena

The Arctic is a land of icy silence, bound by an almost cosmic cold. The ruler of this country is an untiring wanderer born in the snows — the polar bear. Its natural element is ice hummocks and water. The polar bear is at home in the water, swimming freely and seeing beneath the surface, easily leaping across blocks of ice up to two metres in height. A strong and lonely beast, the polar bear does not gather in packs.

Wrangel Island produces the greatest number of cubs. Up to three hundred she-bears den every autumn. Mother bears and their young take their exercise in the archipelagos of Franz Josef Land, Severnaya Zemlya and the Taimyr coast.

633

634

635

636

of these towns in the conditions of permafrost and icy winds blowing from the ocean is an heroic and epic example of man overcoming the forces of nature.

Washed by the Laptev and East Siberian Seas, Yakutia (republic of Sakha) lies in the north-east of Siberia. More than one third of its territory lies inside the Arctic Circle. Most of the republic is occupied by wide mountainous ranges, plateaux and tableland rich in diamonds, gold, tin, mica, tungsten, coal and natural gas. The Lena and Kolyma are the two largest rivers of Yakutia. There are more than seven hundred lakes in the region. The Arctic fox, sable, ermine, fox, northern reindeer, elk, pink seagull and white crane live in Yakutia. The capital of the republic of Sakha is Yakutsk, which lies on the left bank of the River Lena. The town hosts the country's only institute for the study of permafrost.

637

638

The non-urban population of Taimyr is not large and consists of no more than forty-six thousand people – Russians, Dolgans, Nenets, Nganasans, Evenks and Enetses. The basis of their economic activities is reindeer farming, pelt trading, animal breeding (blue and black fox) and fishing. The Evenks are the largest ethnic group inhabiting the Russian polar region. Over thirty thousand Evenks are scattered throughout Central and Eastern Siberia. Their alphabet was created in Latin script in 1931 and Cyrillic script in 1937. Migration has contributed to the formation of different economic and cultural types – hunters, deer breeders and horse breeders. The main branches of the Evenk economy are hunting for ungulate and fur-bearing animals, seasonal fishing and breeding taiga reindeer for transport, determining their semi-nomadic and nomadic way of life. The Dolgans only emerged as an

633. View of Norilsk from a helicopter
634, 635. Yakutia diamonds
636. Ice patterns
637. Polar bear
638. Settlement in the Arctic Circle
639. Monument to Norwegian explorer Peter Tessem in Taimyr
640. River Nakta in the Putoran Plateau
641, 642. Yakutsk
643. Head of a mammoth found in permafrost in Yukagir in Yakutia
644. Yakutsk Museum of the History and Culture of the Peoples of the North
645. River Yana in Yakutia
646. Soil erosion in Yakutia
647. Blessing the Ysyakh festival in Yakutia

Taimyr is home to the world's largest population of northern reindeer. When the spring ice begins to flow at the start of May and the sun stays in the sky for days on end, erasing the border between night and day, the reindeer begin their annual migration northwards. With the dawning of autumn, following the same routes trodden for centuries, thousands of reindeer return across the plateau to spend the winter. The hardy and reliable reindeer are the priceless wealth of the Arctic region. As reindeer breeders lead a nomadic lifestyle, the animals can only feed themselves on each grazing ground once every ten years. Vegetation grows so slowly in the tundra that the reindeer breeders have to annually move their herds in search of food.

648, 649, 652. There are no roads in the tundra. The main form of transport is reindeer, dog sledge, or helicopter.

648

649

650

651

652

653

654

ethnic group in the seventeenth to nineteenth centuries, as a result of the mixing and merging of other groups of nationalities – Evenks (Tunguses), Yankuts, Enetses (Samoyeds) and Russians ("tundra peasants"). They imbibed elements of the culture of their neighbours – the Evenks and the Nganasans. Today, around seven thousand Dolgans live in compact groups in the settlements of Khatanga and Dudinka districts and the town of Dudinka. They continue to engage in reindeer breeding, which is also linked to their main forms of folk creativity – carving on reindeer and mammoth bones, manufacturing clothes and shoes from reindeer fur decorated with beads

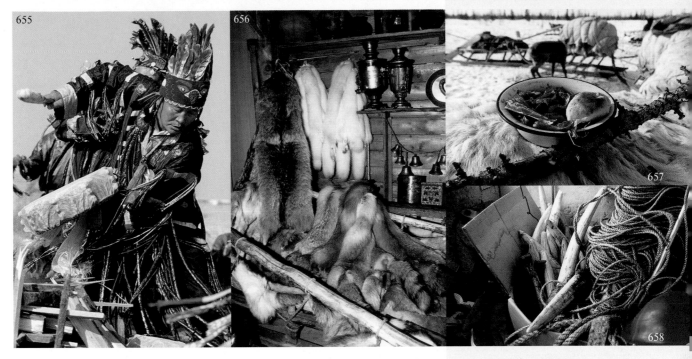

655

656

657

658

and the production of domestic utensils for their nomadic way of life. The northernmost group in the Russian Federation is the Nganasans. Only numbering around 1,200 people, they live in the Taimyr tundra, inside the 72nd parallel. They are descended from the ancient Paleo-Asiatic population of Taimyr, who mixed with the Samoyedic and Tungus tribes. The traditional activities of the Nganasans are hunting, breeding reindeer and fishing. They are masters of the art of carving on mammoth bone, incrustation and stamping of metal, dyed leather and patterned embroideries made from reindeer mane. The Nganasans calculate time according to their own lunar calendar (*kiteda*). One solar year, therefore, has two *khu* – summer and winter. The Nenets people are an indigenous tribe from northern Europe and northern West and Central Siberia. Their traditional occupations are fishing and hunting fur-bearing animals, deer and wild fowls. They live in collapsible, poled nomad's tents covered in reindeer skins in winter and birch bark in summer. Their outer clothing (*malitsa, sokui*) and footwear (*pimy*) are made from reindeer hides. The Nenets people move about on light, wooden sledges. Their food is venison and fish. The majority of the Nenets people used to follow a nomadic way of life.

650, 651. Constructing a nomad's tent
653, 654. River Yana in Yakutia
655, 659–662. International gathering of peoples of the Arctic Circle in Salekhard in April 1998
656. Local Museum in Salekhard
657, 658. Chukotka still-lifes
663. Yakutia →

659

660

661

662

Siberia is first mentioned in the Mongol chronicles of the thirteenth century. The word appears to descend from the "Sibers" – the name of an Ugric tribe. The Russians first learnt of the existence of extensive lands to the east of the Ural Mountains in the early eleventh century. The Novgorodians had contacts with Siberia in the form of trade and military expeditions; their merchants exchanged iron goods and fabrics for pelts. After the Russian victory over the Golden Horde at Kazan in 1552, Muscovy established close contacts with the Siberian khanate.

In 1574, Ivan the Terrible granted the Stroganovs, a famous family of merchants and salt industrialists, the right to form and send military detachments to Siberia. In 1581, the Stroganovs led a large unit of Cossacks into Siberia. Headed by

664

665

666

667

Siberia is the name for the northernmost part of Asia. Approximately thirteen million square kilometres in size, it constitutes around forty percent of the continent's territory. Siberia is bordered by the Ural Mountains in the west, the Pacific Ocean in the east, the Arctic Ocean in the north and the Kazakh and Mongol steppes in the south. Its climate is a mixture of moderate and cold. The winters are long and the summers are warm but short.

The Siberian river network is based on four great waterways – the Ob, Yenisei, Lena

668

669

670

and Amur. There are other large rivers – Indigirka, Kolyma, Olenek, Khatanga and Yana – and many lakes. The largest is the world-famous Lake Baikal. There are five landscape zones in Siberia – tundra, forest, taiga (more than half its territory), mountain and steppe.

Siberia is the treasure-trove of the Russian economy and home to over ninety percent of the country's natural wealth. Almost 100% of the gold, over 95% of the diamonds, over 70% of the coal and oil and over 90%

of the gas is mined in Siberia. The Bratskaya, Krasnoyarskaya, Ust-Ilimskaya and Sayano-Shushenskaya hydroelectric stations and the aluminium factories of Irkutsk, Bratsk, Sayanogorsk and Krasnoyarsk make an important contribution to the Russian industry. The South Siberian, Baikal-Amur and Tyumen-Nizhnevartovsk Railway Lines run through Siberia.

Siberia has given Russian culture a galaxy of famous writers, including Victor Astafiev, Alexander Vampilov and Valentin Rasputin.

the Cossack ataman Yermak, they attacked and occupied the capital of the Siberian khanate — the town of Kashlyk.

The subsequent annexation of Siberia was a relatively peaceful process. Throughout the seventeenth century, free settlements and monasteries began to appear beyond the Urals. The western gates of Siberia opened to welcome a flood of administrators and settlers.

664, 665, 667. River Lena. Olonkho Epic Land
666, 672. Summer in the taiga
668. River Olenek
669. Brown bear — king of the taiga
670. River Moierokan in Evenkia in Krasnoyarsk Region
671. Ussuri taiga near the River Bikin
673. Ground-squirrel
674. Lazovsky Nature Reserve
675. Valley of the River Kotui

155

While Siberia is open to one and all, with everyone able to manifest their talents, only the strong, the stubborn and the sharp-witted survive. The hard life helped to mould the famous Siberian character. Groups of explorers gradually assimilated Eastern Siberia and the Far East. Despite the harsh climate, lack of roads and impassable taiga, swamps, mountains and tundra, they stubbornly forged their way eastwards, founding the stockade towns of Yenisei, Yakutsk, Nerchinsk and Irkutsk. The lands around and beyond Lake Baikal, Chukotka and Kamchatka were actively assimilated. Vladimir Atlasov, Pyotr Beketov, Semyon Dezhnev, Kurbat Ivanov, Yerofei Khabarov, Ivan Moskvitin, Ivan Perfiliev and Vasily Poyarkov are just some of the names to go down in Russian history.

Each Siberian town is unique in its own way. Novosibirsk on the River Ob is the largest cultural, scientific and educational centre, with the largest academic library in Siberia and one of the finest universities in Russia.

The city of Novosibirsk is home to the country's largest theatre of opera and ballet, staging productions by famous directors and designers.

Tyumen is the first Russian city in Siberia. Founded as a stockade town on the banks of the River Tura (a tributary of the Tobol) in the seventeenth century, it was an important transit point on the trade route to Cathay. The close relationship between the landscape and architecture reflects the deep roots of Russian culture in Tyumen. The nineteenth-century house carvings are particularly famous.

685

Krasnoyarsk Region stretches from the shores of the Arctic Ocean to the sun-scorched steppes of Khakasia and the snowy peaks of the Sayan Mountains. It is transversed from south to north by one of the mightiest Russian rivers — the Yenisei. The second-longest river in Siberia, the Yenisei receives the waters of over one hundred thousand tributaries. The Evenks called it the River Yonessy ("Large Water"), inspiring its current Russian name. Krasnoyarsk Region is so large that it includes virtually every geographical zone in Russia — steppe, forest, taiga, tundra and Arctic wastes. The administrative centre of the region is the city of Krasnoyarsk. The romantic and austere nature provides a handsome backdrop of green hills, rocky cliffs and the clear waters of the Yenisei, in which the modern, multistorey buildings of the town are reflected. Vasily Surikov was born and lived in Krasnoyarsk. His

686

688

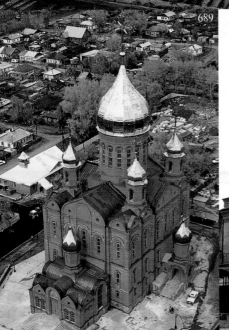

689

687

house on Annunciation Street is now a memorial museum devoted to the famous Russian artist.

Tobolsk, the historical capital of Siberia, was constructed at the confluence of the Tobol and the Irtysh. The traditional craft of bone carving continues to develop in the town, thanks to the abundance of mammoth tusk in West Siberia and the knowledge of the art of carving of the native tribes. Tobolsk is also home to the first Siberian kremlin or citadel.

690

676. Tyumen. Kremlin (founded in 1586)
677. Province Administration of Tyumen
678. Tyumen. "Zasibgazprom"
679. Tobolsk. Kremlin
680. Novosibirsk. Opera and Ballet Theatre
681. Fireworks in Krasnoyarsk
682. Omsk. Russian Drama Theatre
683. Omsk. Irtysh Embankment
684. Bridge over the River Irtysh
685. Krasnoyarsk. Intercession Cathedral. 18th century
686. Krasnoyarsk. River Yenisey
687. River Irtysh. Timber-rafting
688. Krasnoyarsk Province. River Podkamennaya Tunguska
689. Kemerovo. Cathedral of the Icon of the Mother of God of the Sign. 1996
690. Tomsk. Monument to Anton Tchekhov. 2004. Sculptor L. Usov

157

Siberia is a specific "crossroads" of civilisations, representing a successful example of the interaction of different nationalities, cultures and religions throughout its history (particularly in the Russian period). Recent centuries have witnessed the stable growth of the place and role of Siberia in Russian life. Siberia is home to over ninety percent of the country's natural wealth. The Altai is an original crossroads of civilisa-

The Altai (from the Mongolian word *altain* for "golden") is a mountainous country in the centre of Asia, on the territory of Russia, Kazakhstan, Mongolia and China. It consists of a system of steep and inaccessible ridges forming the watershed of the Ob, Irtysh and Yenisei and the rivers of the basin of Central Asia. The highest peak of the Altai is the legendary Mount Belukha (4,506 metres). Sayany is a mountainous land in south Siberia, consisting of the mountain systems of West and East Sayan.

Travellers were drawn to the rivers Katun, Biya and Chuya and the multitude of lakes. The largest and most famous is Lake Teletskoe ("Golden Lake"), whose waters are particular clear and pure. Fir, cedar-fir, spruce and pine trees grow in the forests of Altai and Sayany. Some cedars grow to an age of six hundred years. The area is inhabited by the musk deer, brown bear, lynx, glutton and even the extremely rare snow leopard, listed in the Red Book of endangered and protected species. The Russian share of the Altai is rich in deposits of mercury, gold, iron and marble. Mountain crystal and gems represent great value.

The spread of Russian statehood in the Altai began with the transformations of Peter the Great. In 1729, industrialist Akinfy Demidov founded the Kolyvansky-Voskresensky Copper-Smelting works. Under Empress Elizabeth Petrovna, the Altai mountain district produced industrial silver. Elizabeth

tions — historical, cultural and archaeological. Many different cultures and nations sprung up in this region, influencing the subsequent fates of other territories. A unique fusion of antiquity and modernity, Asian colourfulness and Russian enterprise, the Altai was an important cultural and historical centre. Scythian culture developed here in the first millennium BC, giving world history a whole series of remarkable works of art. The first archaeological expeditions took place during the reign of Peter the Great in the early eighteenth century. The discoveries

commanded that the first cast at the Barnaul Silver-Refining Works be made for the tombstone of St Alexander Nevsky. This work is now on exhibition in the Hermitage Museum. The famous "queen of vases" was fashioned at the Kolyvansky Stone Cutting Works.

The ethnographic diversity of the peoples of the south and north Altai was formed on the different material bases and geographic conditions of the Altai-Sayan tableland. The culture and way of life of the southern Altai people were shaped by their nomadic and semi-nomadic traditions of cattle breeding

and grazing. As with the peoples of the northern Altai, they were formed over the centuries on the basis of animal hunting, taiga gathering, fishing and hoe-mattock farming.

Many glorious deeds and names are linked to the Altai region. These range from Ivan Polzunov's invention of the world's first steam engine to the space flights of such cosmonauts from the Altai as Gherman Titov and Vasily Lazarev. The region has produced many leading people of culture, including the talented writer, actor and director Vasily Shukshin.

made in the burial mounds offer a fascinating insight into the art of the Altai nomads. The most interesting objects are the works of gold — necklaces, buckles and images of animals — now in the collections of the Hermitage Museum in St Petersburg, the History Museum in Moscow and museums in Stockholm. Also of exceptional interest are the unique fabrics and rugs — the earliest evidence of the existence of weaving and the art of carpet making in the Middle East.

691. Belukha Nature Preserve
692, 695, 699. Mountain lakes
693, 694, 696, 698. River Katoun
697. Altai Mountains
700. Altai. Waterfalls
701. Altai. River Chuya
702. Altai landscape →

703
704
705
706
707

The waters of Lake Baikal have remarkable properties. They contain high levels of oxygen and low doses of minerals. Even at a depth of forty feet, they are distinguished for their great transparency. The flora and fauna of Baikal include around 2,600 different species, three quarters of which can only be found in the lake — Baikal omul, oilfish, yellowfin sculpin and nerpa or Baikal seal.

703. Lake Baikal
704. Baikal is a unique fishing ground. Fifty-two species inhabit the lake, seventeen of which are of commercial importance, including the omul, sturgeon, umber, taimen, dace, burbot, pike and lenok.
705. River Angara

708

Baikal is the deepest lake in the world. Located in Buryatia and Irkutsk Region in the south of East Siberia, its depth reaches 1,620 metres. Baikal is one of the ten largest lakes in the world (its size is 31,500 square kilometres). Twenty or thirty million years old, it is the oldest freshwater reservoir on the planet. The lake is the world's largest depository of fresh water – twenty-three thousand cubic kilometres or one fifth of the total supply. Baikal contains as much water as all five great lakes of North America combined.

709

710

706. Pikes
707, 708. Lake Baikal. Pestchanaya Bay
709. Irkutsk. Monument to Alexander III
     (Replica of Robert Bach's statue
     of 1904)
710. Lake Baikal. Village Listvianka
711. Baikal landscape
712, 713. Irkutsk. Details of wooden
     dwelling decor
714. Kazak Tower. Detail

The unique beauty of Baikal and its shores make it one of the most majestic natural monuments on earth. The picturesque shores are lined with conifer forests, the towns of Slyudyanka, Baikalsk, Severobaikalsk and Babushkin and the ports and settlements of Kultuk, Tankhoi, Baikal, Vydrino, Ust-Barguzin and Lower Angarsk. The north-east section of the lake lies within the Barguzinsky Reserve, the south shore is part of the Baikal Reserve, while the west shore belongs to the Pribaikal National Park and Baikal-Lena Reserve. Although 336 rivers fall into Lake Baikal, the largest of which are the Selenga, Barguzin, Turka and Snezhnaya, only one flows out of it. This is the River Angara, which starts life as a powerful current, before developing into a cascade of reservoirs. Rushing on its multi-kilometre path, carrying the power, purity and transparency of the Baikal waters through majestic valleys, the river is an unforgettable sight.

Valuable deposits of iron, magnesium, mica and coal have been discovered in the Angara basin. Many treasures, however, remain unknown. Experts have calculated that there are a billion cubic metres of rare wood in the Angara taiga.

711

712

713

714

Eastern Siberia covers an enormous territory, stretching for two thousand miles from west to east, from the River Yenisei to the Stanovoi Range. It is only slightly smaller in size than the United States of America (without Alaska). The nature of Eastern Siberia is more diverse than that of Western Siberia. The reason is its enormous size and predomination of plateaux and mountainous regions. Eastern Siberia contains enormous spaces with still unassimilated lands and vast mineral, forest and hydroelectric resources. In the south of East Siberia, there is a mountainous territory adjoining Lake Baikal from the east — Zabaikalye. One of its components is the republic of Buryatia. The southern part of East Siberia has another republic called Tuva (Tyva). According to the republic's new constitution (2001),

715

716

717

Zabaikalye (literally "beyond Baikal") is a large territory covering the mountain ranges in the southern part of Eastern Siberia, adjoining Lake Baikal from the east. One of the regions of Zabaikalye is the republic of Buryatia, which includes the Zabaikalsky and Tunkinsky National Parks and the Barguzinsky and Dzherginsky Reserves. Buryatia is a mountainous area. The southern districts of the republic are the most densely populated, particularly the valley and sources of the River Selenga. Up to forty percent of the population is composed of Buryat Mongols, who live everywhere, but predominate on the left bank of the Selenga. Evenks settled in the northern districts; Soiots (Tuvintsy) are also encountered in Buryatia. The towns, workers settlements and the villages on the right bank of the River Selenga are dominated by Russians. The native inhabitants only moved from a nomadic to a settled way of life in the Soviet period, creating thousands of new settlements (uluses) and considerably increasing the number of urban dwellers.

The capital of Buryatia, Ulan-Ude, lies in the valley of the River Selenga. The town was founded in 1666 as the Cossack winter quarters of Udginskoe for the collection of tributes from the Evenks and Buryats. The largest cultural centre of the republic, Ulan-Ude is home to the Buryat Theatre of Opera and Ballet, the Buryat Theatre of Drama and the Russian Drama Theatre.

The republic of Tuva (Tyva) or, as it was called in olden times, Tannu-Tuva ("land of the blue river"), has an interesting history. It is located in the south of Eastern Siberia. In the Middle Ages, the territory of Tannu-Tuva was part of the Turkic and Uigursk kaganates. It was conquered by the Mongols in the thirteenth century and the Manchuri-

718

the names of Tuva and Tyva are of equal standing. The Republic of Tuva is the youngest entity in the Russian Federation and a signatory to the Siberian Agreement interregional association.

715. Foothills of Sayany in Buryatia
716, 718. Aginsky Datsan in Buryatia
717. Pilgrims on the site of a ruined temple in Buryatia
719. Steppe in Tuva
720. River Yenisei
721. Team of steppe horses in Tuva
722. Herd of sarlyks in Tuva
723. Sayan Mountains
724. Buryat girls
725. Chita
726. Buryat folk dance
727. Petroglyphs in Kyzyl

ans in the seventeenth century. In the eighteenth century, it was colonised by Russian merchants, explorers, runaway serfs and Old Believers fleeing the oppression of the Orthodox Church. The Tannu-Tuva people hunted and bred reindeer. Under the influence of the Russians, they began to till the soil and breed cattle.

The republic of Tuva is divided into sixteen administrative districts and has five large towns – Kyzyl, Ak-Dovurak, Turan, Chadan and Shagonar.

The capital of Tuva, Kyzyl, lies at the confluence of two rivers – Large Yenisei (By-Khem) and Small Yenisei (Ka-Khem), forming the Upper Yenisei (Ulug-Khem). Geographically, Kyzyl stands at the very centre of Asia. Tourists always visit the famous *Centre of Asia* obelisk. Other attractions include the theatre of music and drama, philharmonic hall and the museum of local studies. Near Kyzyl, on the right bank of the Upper Yenisei, are caves with unique wall inscriptions and drawings.

The Far East federal district stretches from Vladivostok to Petropavlovsk-Kamchatsky. It includes Amur, Kamchatka, Magadan and Sakhalin Regions, the Jewish Autonomous Region, Koryaksky and Chukotka autonomous districts, Maritime and Khabarovsk regions and the Republic of Sakha (Yakutia), which is sometimes regarded as part of Siberia.

The Far East is one of the most unique corners on earth for the countless treasures of its soil and the magical wealth of its flora and fauna. It is home to ninety different

728

729

730

731

732

The westernmost part of the Russian Far East, the mountainous Amur Region is located in the basin of the rivers Amur and Zeya. It borders Khabarovsk Region to the west. Its enormous territory is washed by the Sea of Okhotsk and the Sea of Japan. Mixed forests grow in the south; further north, the taiga spreads and tundra is encountered. Among the numerous rivers of this region are the Tunguska and Ussuri. Much of the land is covered by the mountain ranges of Sikhote-Alinya and Dzhugdzhura.

The administrative centre of Amur Region and oldest population point in the Far East is Blagoveschensk, which was founded in 1856. The city of Khabarovsk was founded two years later and named in honour of explorer Yerofei Khabarov. The Khabarovsk Region also boasts the ports of Vanino, Nikolaevsk-on-Amur and Okhotsk.

The pearl of the Maritime Region is Vladivostok – the largest town in the Russian Far East and the terminus of the Trans-Siberian Railway. Nestling on the shore of the Pacific Ocean, Vladivostok perches like an amphitheatre on the hills at the southern end of the Muravyov-Amur Peninsula. All city streets lead to the picturesque harbour of the Golden Horn, which shields the town from the Pacific winds. The Maritime Region is located where the Eurasian land-

733

734

mammals and four hundred species of birds, twenty-seven of which are included in the Red Book of endangered and protected species. The rivers and lakes abound with over a hundred species of fish. The Far East is the homeland of the lotus, the cedar and the legendary root of life or ginseng.

728, 731–733. Vladivostok
729. Khabarovsk. Transfiguration Cathedral
730. Khabarovsk's new dwellings
734–736, 739. Magadan Region
737. Ussuri taiga at the River Bikin

735

736

737

738. Peter the Great Bay
740. The Maritime Region is also home to the main population of the Amur tiger — the largest predator of the cat family. The actions of poachers, who sell animal skins and bones for use in traditional medicines, have reduced the number of tigers living wild in the Far East to no more than four hundred. Every measure is now being taken to save this endangered species.
741. Virgin stone birch forest

738

739

mass meets the Pacific Ocean. Besides the mainland, its composition includes numerous islands. The original climate of this land and amplitude of the relief create a unique natural environment sometimes known as the "northern jungle" for the exotic combinations of vegetation, in which southern lianas often wind around northern firs.

The natural riches of the Far East are countless. The soil abounds in rock miner-als, including gold. The Maritime Region is the only area in Russia inhabited by the leopard. Ussuri tigers live amid the haunting natural beauty of the Khertsirsky Reserve. The waters are the Mecca of all Russian anglers. The shoreline is also famed for its rich catches. Seals, sea lions and white whales are encountered in the waters. The Trans-Siberian and Baikal-Amur Railway Lines run through the territory.

740

741

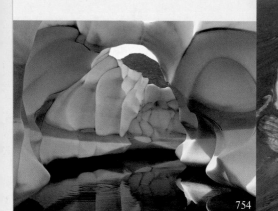

754

755

Kamchatka, a magic land of wildlife wonders, is a peninsula in far eastern Russia, lying between the Sea of Okhotsk on the west and the Pacific Ocean and Bering Sea on the east. It is about 1,200 km long north-south and about 480 km across at its widest. The climate of the Kamchatka Peninsula is severe, with prolonged, cold, and snowy winters and wet, cool summers.

754. Glacial cave in Chashakondzha
755. Aerial shot of a crater.
   Kamchatka attracts many tourists from different countries of the world with its snow-covered mountains and broad gulfs, green forests and sheltered lowlands.

Kamchatka boasts of unique landscapes, fantastic beauty and striking contrasts of relief and temperatures. The area abounds with mountain ranges and extensive valleys, plain rivers and vast swamps, hot and cold springs. Klyuchevskaya Volcano is one of the highest active volcanoes in the world. It consists of a truncated cone with a central crater, with some lateral craters and cones on the lower slopes. In the eighteenth and nineteenth centuries, the volcano exploded over fifty times, continuing to rumble throughout the twentieth century. It was particularly violent in 1944 and 1980. Lava erupted with a thunderous bang, volcanic bombs flew up into the air and the ground shook over an area of several hundred square miles. After the last eruption, a crack formed on the slope of the volcano. Extending for almost a mile, it spewed out lava and ash. Of the 160 volcanoes, 30 are still active, as are a number of geysers, underground steam and hot springs.

Other highlight of the peninsula is the Valley of the Geysers, a profound canyon with 20 big geysers and a lot of pulsating, bubbling and boiling springs. A geyser is a type of hot spring that erupts periodically, ejecting a column of hot water and steam into the air. Geyser activity is caused by surface water seeping down through the ground until it meets rock heated by magma. Steam then sprays out of the geyser. Each geyser has its own name, reflecting

756

757

758

760

756. Uzon Caldera
757. Stone birch is the main tree
of the Kamchatka mountainous
forests.
758. Mount Karymsky
759. Valley of the Geysers, a profound
canyon with geysers and a lot
of pulsating, bubbling and boiling
springs.
760. Key (Klyuchevskaya Sopka)
and Flat Near (Cross) Volcanoes
761, 765. Eruption of Mount Karymsky
762. Avachinskaya Harbour. Three
Brothers Cliff
763. Mud volcano
764. Bubbles in a mud volcano

759

its specific features — Triple, Cone, Sugar, Pearl, Big Stove, Fissure or Horizontal. The impression produced by this phenomenon of nature is only comparable to such wonders of the world as the Grand Canyon and the Niagara Falls in North America, Lake Baikal in Siberia and the Great Barrier Reef in Australia. Petropavlovsk-Kamchatsky is the only town on the peninsula founded on the site of the Kamchadal settlement of Aushin. On 6/17 October 1740, the Kamchatka expedition of Vitus Bering and Alexei Chirikov stopped to spend the winter here (the town was named after their two ships — *St Peter* and *St Paul*).

761

762

763 764

765

LIFE AND TRADITIONS, RELIGION, COUNTRY AND PEOPLE

Every civilisation is unique and chooses its own path. Every culture has its own ways, connected both to geographical factors and living conditions. What do we know about the Russian character and the spirit of the Russian people? We will try to answer this question.

766

767

In ancient times, the territory of Russia was inhabited by such Eastern Slavic tribes as the Polan, Drevlyane, Ulich, Tiverets, Vyatich, Dregovich and Ilmen Slavs. The modern population of Russia is mostly descended from these tall, handsome, strapping men and women. Much has been passed down through the ages and generations, retained in our physical appearances, characters, habits and customs. Our ancestors tilled the soul (bread was their main food), bred cattle, hunted, fished and kept bees. They were pagans and worshipped the gods of the sun (known as Dazbog, Jarilo or Hors), wind (Stribog) and thunder (Perun). The end of the frosts signalled widespread festivities, seeing off the winter and greeting the spring. People baked round pancakes symbolising the sun and burnt straw effigies of winter.

The Russian Orthodox Church has been the most important factor shaping the minds of the nation. The profound religious beliefs of the Russian people explain such features as their great patience in arduous situations, sense of conscience, kindness and compassion towards their fellow man, strivings for the spiritual and mistrust of cold calculation, personal advantage and mercantilism. Although our troubled history has inevitably altered the national character, the aforementioned qualities still live on in the leading representatives of the nation. Russia is a country of firm and steady traditions. A special atmosphere of cordiality arises whenever close friends and relatives gather for refreshments or conversation. Russians living abroad generally miss this special sense of spiritual community.

Drinking tea with spice cakes, gingerbread, biscuits, pies and pancakes is a Russian national custom. There is something magically enchanting about sitting around the samovar with a steaming cup of tea. Heated by charcoal, every real samovar has its own unique voice — a calming melody coming straight from its heart, forming the perfect background to the partaking of tea. The character of the Russian people is reflected in its love of festivities, accompanied by mass gatherings, traditional games, singing, dancing and other forms of entertainment.

766. Traditional household objects
767. St Petersburg cabbies in a teahouse. Late 1860s. Photograph
768. Russian troika
769. WWII veteran
770. The stove is the heart of the Russian house. Like a mother, it feeds, warms, cleans, provides a bed and heals ailments.
771. Bread is the head of everything!
772. Siberian hunter

773

774

Christmas merges naturally with New Year. Christmas Eve is celebrated on 6 January and known as *sochelnik*, from the name of the ritual fare — *sochivo*. Carol-singers dress up and go round all the houses in the village, praising the birth of the Saviour. The decoration of Christmas trees, giving of presents and Yuletide fortune telling make this one of the merriest religious holidays. Throughout the twelve days of Christmas, people pay visits to friends and relatives and receive guests at home. Rich people held masked balls, carnivals and charity banquets. The central focus of all winter festivities was the hospitable table. In olden days, the table was scattered with hay — in memory of the Bethlehem manger — and then laid with a snow-white tablecloth. The Christmas meal

775

776

The Shrovetide rituals have pagan roots. Saying farewell to the departing winter, greeting the long-awaited spring and the arrival of the larks — all this was reflected in the boisterous Shrovetide festivities, featuring troika rides, the taking of snow towns, the building of ice houses and fist fights. Pancakes stuffed with berries, mushrooms, salted fish and salmon or sturgeon caviar are the main food on the Shrovetide table, the hot hors d'oeuvres accompanying the vodka.

773. Snow Maiden, granddaughter of
      Father Christmas, in Veliky Ustyug
774—776, 781. Shrovetide in full swing
777, 778. Celebrating Trinity
779, 780. Christmas holidays
782, 783. Celebrating Victory Day

had twelve courses — pancakes, fish, aspic, galantine, milk piglet, pig's head with radish, homemade sausage, roast meat, honey cake, poppy seed and honey pastries and baking. The central religious festival in Russia is Easter, which is celebrated with a special piety and joy, accompanied by many historical customs. Russian housewives begin their preparations on Maundy Monday, the first day in the last week of Lent. On Holy Thursday, people paint eggs, make *paskha* and bake *kulich*. These obligatory culinary masterpieces of the Easter meal are consecrated in church and decorated with flowers. Many other dishes are cooked for the celebratory dinner, including lamb, roast beef and ham. Easter lasts for an entire week, during which the table remains set for all invited and uninvited guests.

Bathing in a hole in the ice is linked to Old Russian Orthodox tradition. Epiphany, which celebrates the baptism of Jesus Christ in the River Jordan, coincided with a period of hard frosts in Russia. On frozen rivers and lakes, holes were made in the ice and called "jordans" in memory of this

One of the most popular Russian customs is visiting a bathhouse (*banya*). Vladimir Dahl's *Explanatory Dictionary* claims that the word comes from the verb *banit'* (to wash or clean with water). In the Russian bathhouse, people "wash and soak themselves in both the dry heat and steam vapours." In the early eighteenth century, a traveller wrote: "Russians are as accustomed to washing in the bathhouse as they are to food and drink. They use the bathhouse as a form of treating any ailment."

Traditional Russian bathhouses were built from wooden logs. The construction of stone bathhouses only began in the nineteenth century, when urban public bathhouses became widespread. Inside, the bathhouse is divided into two parts — the changing room and the steam room. This layout still survives today. The traditional procedure

for visiting a bathhouse was formed over the centuries. First of all, the men experienced the main or "hellish" heat, followed by the women and children. People also visited the bathhouse as a family unit. Steaming was as important as washing. This was done with the help of birch besoms, used to lash the naked skin. Hot water was sprinkled onto the stove, often mixed with bread kvas or aromatic grass extracts. The bathhouse was

an important element in the wedding ceremony. Pre-nuptial ablutions were held in the houses of both the bride and the groom, symbolising the purification of the marriage. Even the Russian aristocracy and sovereigns used the bathhouse during the wedding ceremony, both for washing and for a banquet. Fist fights were held on Shrovetide, the week preceding the start of Lent. These contests were popular among young men in Russia.

event. After the blessing of the waters, many Russians braved the freezing temperatures and entered the water for the traditional Epiphany ablution. This tradition is currently enjoying a revival.

784, 787. Everything for the bathhouse
785. Local inhabitants in a Russian bathhouse in Ivanovo Region
786, 788–790. "Steam does not break bones..."
791. Changing room of a Russian bathhouse in winter
792, 794. Straight out into the frost
793. After the bathhouse
795. "Snow-bathing" in Ivanovo Region — Russian winter bathhouse tradition
796. Dousing in icy water
797. Seeing off winter in Oryol
798. Swimming in a hole in the ice

799

800

Fishing is one of the most popular pastimes of the Russian people. As elsewhere in the world, angling has ceased to be a means of acquiring food and gradually turned into a cult or form of meditation. There are many excellent fishing grounds in the Russian Federation. The Mecca of anglers, however, is the unique natural complex of the Volga-Akhtuba basin and the delta of the River Volga. During the spring spawning, vobla, bream, sea roach, crucian, rudd, pike, perch, aspius, sazan, catfish, ide, tench, carp and white salmon all return here to their natural breeding grounds from the Caspian Sea. Fish can also be caught in the summer, after the waters have abated, and during their autumn movement. Bites follow one after another, not allowing an angler a minute's relaxation. Other attractive fishing grounds are the rivers of the Kola Pen-

801

802

insula, which abound in salmon and trout, and the forest streams and lakes of north Karelia and Lake Onega, which are famed for their umber, white fish, pike and perch. The White Sea offers both coastal and deep-sea fishing for salmon, cod, lancet and bass. There is excellent fishing in the Siberian rivers (taimen, pike, umber, burbot and lenoc) and, of course, Lake Baikal (home to fifty-two species of freshwater fish). Kamchatka is an Eldorado of all modifications of salmon in the Sea of Okhotsk — Siberian salmon, red salmon, king salmon, silversides, hunchback salmon and loach.

Fishing under the ice is as important as summer angling in a country with such long and arduous winters as Russia. This pastime is particularly challenging and exciting in early spring, when the ice loses its firmness and begins to crack in places.

799. Fishing nets at the Kizhi Museum Complex
800. International angling competition for the Moscow Mayor's Cup on the River Moscow
801. Ice fishing on the Gulf of Finland near St Petersburg
802. Everyone is a fisherman in Vladivostok
803. Four-legged fish fan
804. Perches
805. Catching sterlets
806. Bolshoi Peles Island in the Sea of Japan
807. On a bridge in Kirillov
808. Fisherwoman
809. Politician Vladimir Zhirinovky with a sturgeon
810. Winter fishing on the Volga
811. Fisherman's soup. Tikhaya Bay in Kamchatka

Forty-five percent of Russia is covered in woodland, mostly coniferous, with over 1,500 species of trees and shrubs. The forests are rich in wildlife, including fur-bearing animals. The majority of natural resources are concentrated in sparsely populated regions — northern Russia, Siberia and the Far East. Hunting as a source of food is one of the oldest activities of mankind and enjoyed a special place in Old Russia. As an original lifestyle, however, Russian hunting is a relatively young phenomenon. Its history can only be traced

Hunting was both a necessity of life and a popular pastime in Russia. In terms of their mastery, modern hunters have not advanced much further from their ancient predecessors. Although complex viewing apparatus and high-speed vehicles have appeared, the essence of hunting has not undergone any cardinal changes among professionals.

Hunting forges the character, develops strength and stamina, cultivates focus and fearlessness and encourages a disregard of both heat and cold. Hunters acquire such important qualities as an agile step, lightness of movement and instant reactions. Hunting develops a command of weapons — shooting from a rifle or wielding a knife or spear — training the mind and hand. Knowledge of various ruses and the ability to set traps, snares and nooses also contribute to success in hunting.

Hunting was traditionally one of the most popular pastimes in Russia. Nobles, princes and tsars all hunted, while their numerous vassals and servants also took part in this truly masculine activity, which required dexterity, courage and indefatigability. The tsar Alexis, Peter the Great's father, enjoyed hunt-

back a thousand years, although its roots go back much further. "Hunting deserves to be considered one of the main activities of man. Since time immemorial, Russians have enjoyed hunting. This is reflected in our songs, our sagas and all our legends." These words were written by Ivan Turgenev, the author of Sketches from a Hunter's Album *and an incorrigible hunter all his life. His passion was shared by many other famous Russian writers, including Leo Tolstoy, Nikolai Nekrasov and Ivan Bunin, who all wrote works about hunting.*

812. Fox
813. Hunter in the Maritime Region
814. Siberian hunter with trophies
815. Lynx
816. Hunting in Magadan Region

ing, particularly falconry. He kept over 3,000 falcons and a 100,000 pigeon nests to provide them with fresh meat. After the Peter's death (the tsar himself didn't like hunting) the Imperial Hunts became popular in Russia during the second quarter of the 18th century, they were an important part of Imperial Court life. Peter II and Elizabeth Petrovna were fond of hounds of venery, while Alexander II, Alexander III and Nicholas II preferred rifle hunting. Hunting gradually became less exclusive in the nineteenth century, when it attracted members of all Russian classes.

In hunting, the game can be animals or birds. Hunting bears or hares and falconry were popular national pastimes in Russia. Bear hunting was a form of single combat, involving the spear, knife or hounds. Foxes and wolves were often baited as an attraction. Spectators admired the swiftness and fury of the dogs. Falconry was a particularly refined sport. The sight of birds of prey engaging in duels with other birds high in the sky was a magnificent spectacle. Hunting boars and elks was widespread in Russia. Before the revolution, the tsars hunted bison.

817, 822. Hunting in the mountains
     of the Maritime Region
818. Arctic fox
819. Elk
820. Bear – king of the forest
821. Grouse
823. Wolf
824, 827. With game
825. Spaniel
826. Hunter in a Siberian lodge

830

828

The Handbook for the Experienced Russian Housewife (1845) contains the following justified statement: "Without putting down German or French cuisine, I think that, for us, in all respects, there is nothing healthier or better than our own native Russian food, to which we are used and accustomed, derived from the experience of the centuries, handed down from fathers to children and justified by our geographical location, climate and lifestyle."

The tradition of serving starters or *hors d'œuvres* is said to have arisen in Russia. Life itself dictated the order of Russian meals. The

831

832

829

833

834

835

836

828–830, 832, 836. In addition to distinctly national specialties such as caviar, salted, jerked and smoked or dried dishes, bread, present-day *zakuskas* in a general sense have included West European, meat-jellies, sandwiches, salads and seafood.

831, 837, 838. Tea-drinking with honey cakes, gingerbread, pies, cookies and *blinis* is a national custom popular in every Russian household.

833. Shashlyk

834. After *shchi* and *kasha*, *pelmeni* (pasta poaches) are perhaps the most popular Russian dish.

835. Stocked up products are a good help for a housewife, especially when the season of fresh vegetables is over and your table needs a variety. Then comes the time of foodstuffs kept in stock.

839, 840. You are welcome!

837

838

839

harsh climate taught people to keep all possible stores of food at home as a guarantee of survival. This explains why fish, meat, poultry and game were salted, pickled and kept in abundance. The traditional Russian starters are caviar, cured and smoked fish and meat dishes. The main courses are heated — rich and nourishing cabbage and fish soups — supplemented by various forms of pasties. Meat, fish and vegetable pasties are the first refreshments and traditional starters in Russian houses, both on everyday and special occasions.

One of the staple Russian fares has always been *kasha* or porridge, which also has a ritual significance. It was eaten to celebrate the birth of a new baby or to remember the dead. The bride and groom cooked porridge at their wedding, leading to the popular expression "you won't cook porridge with him or her."

Bread and grain are the two main foodstuffs in Russia, reflected in such national adages as "buckwheat porridge is our mother and rye bread is our father" and "borsch without kasha is a widower and kasha without borsch is a widow."

After cabbage soup and porridge, the third most popular food in Russia is probably *pelmeni* (dumplings). The staple food of the inhabitants of the Urals and Siberia, they are filled with meat, fish, mushrooms or potatoes.

841

842

The everyday lives of the Russian people were surrounded by genuine creativity. Special attention was paid to the construction and decoration of houses. As forests grew everywhere, the most accessible building material was wood. Carpenters and carvers found it an easy medium to work with, creating a solid and handsome pattern.

Domestic fretwork was popular in the traditional decor of the Russian peasant hut. The pediments of wooden houses still retain the heads of horses, cockerels or other birds and grapnel boards along the slopes of the roof. The frames of windows, balconies and porches were also decorated with slits.

Wood was widely employed in the manufacture of crockery and utensils — scoops, buckets, barrels, baskets, bowls, boxes, cylinders, distaffs, furniture, sleighs, carts and harnesses. These objects were covered in three-dimensional, relief and flat fretwork, coloured and patterned. Young birch bark was also used in Russia for the manufacture of household objects. Punnets, barrels, baskets, boxes and bread-bins were then deco-

843

rated with stamping, lace fretwork or paint-work, while bast shoes were plaited. A skilled craftsman could transform a tree bark into a masterpiece of art.

Clay and the potter's wheel were another traditional medium and technique in Russia. Clay vessels were fired in kilns and decorated with simple ornamentation. Russian artisans created enormous vessels for holding water, large earthenware tankards, pots, cream jugs and milk churns.

The Russian peasant experienced an inexplicable and insurmountable need for beauty. All items created by the Russian peasantry, therefore, combined utilitarian convenience with aesthetic charms. The name of the famous Khokhloma brand is derived

841. Birch bark plaiting in Malovishersky District, Novgorod Region
842. Wooden crockery. 1980s. Pskov. Master N. Stepanov
843. Plaiting bast shoes
844. Wood carver in Semino, Nizhny Novgorod Region
845. Building a wooden hut in Schelykovo, Kostroma Region
846, 847. Carved window frames and horses — traditional Russian house decorations
848. Ceramicist working on a potter's wheel in Pskov
849. Watermill. Miller. Opochinsky District, Pskov Region
850. Trays and spoons. Pskov wood carver N. Stepanov

Arising in the east a thousand years ago, the art of the varnished miniature acquired bright national features in Mstiora, Palekh, Fedoskino and Kholui. Despite the stylistic originality of each centre, they all employ a common technology of production. Sheets of cardboard are pasted together, pressed, dried, soaked with linseed oil, hardened in kilns, primed, polished and varnished to the point of smoothness. A fairytale, literary, national or historical subject or an ornamental composition is then painted in tempera in an icon-painting technique. This design is covered in several coats of light varnish and polished until it shines like a mirror. Painted trays belong to the family of Russian varnished goods. Their production began in the nine-

851

853

854

852

855

856

from the name of a village where merchants bought up painted wooden crockery for delivery to sales of work. The main artistic devices of the Khokhloma technique still survive to this day. Loving cups and stands were fashioned from wood and covered several times in a clay solution, oil and aluminium powder. Rhythmic patterns of ornate golden volutes of leaves and grass were then applied to their bodies, surrounded by images of small red berries. The cups were finally covered in varnish and hardened in a kiln, where the high temperature turned its surface a golden colour.

The artistic centres of Khokhloma are located in Nizhny Novgorod Region. The town of Semyonov also produces the world-famous *matryoshka* or nestling doll. *Matrioshkas* are made here in an unsophisticated manner — four to seven nested dolls with traditional red and yellow painted design and subsequent lacquering. Equally handsome works are created in Polkhovsky Maidan and Sergiev Posad — the traditional home of the *matryoshka* and even a Russian Toy Museum. The geography of the Russian folk toy spreads far and wide, embracing the

857

858

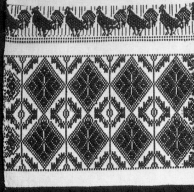
859

teenth century in the village of Zhostovo near Moscow. The objects gradually lost their original domestic purposes, becoming unique works of folk art. A bouquet is usually painted on the black, blue, yellow or red background of the tray. Large flowers are depicted in the centre in bright paints, with smaller, slightly darker flowers emerging from the depths along the edges.

851. S. Veselov, master of Khokhloma painting, in Semino, Nizhny Novgorod Region
852. Leonid Sobinov Memorial Museum, Schelykovo, Kostroma Region
853, 854. Khokhloma souvenirs are famed worldwide for their original beauty.

"bobbies" of Kargopol, the water carriers of Dymkovo and the whistles of Filimonovo.

Embroidery and lacework are two of the most widespread forms of handicraft in Russia. Embroideries decorated costumes, towels, valances and other household items. Russian seamstresses developed a unique form of golden embroidery, used to embellish religious vestments and icons in convents.

Russian lace was prized for its high technical qualities and original ornamentation. The lace craft of Vologda enjoyed international fame. Nowadays, seamstresses embroider military insignia for the army and navy and diverse household goods.

The ancient town of Rostov the Great stands on the high bank of Lake Nero. Its craftsmen are well versed in the secrets of the ancient handicraft known as Russian enamel painting. To this day Rostov artists paint enamel decorations and local jewellers set their enamel plaques into ornate mounts.

860

861

862

863

864

866

865

855. Baking wooden spoons in a kiln in Semino, Nizhny Novgorod Region
856, 864, 866. Masters at work
857. Russian nestling doll. Semyonov, Nizhny Novgorod Region
858. Young master at work in Novgorod
859. Embroidered towel
860. Dymkovo toy: To the Bazaar. Vyatka. Artist L. Ivanova
861. Karelian masters threading beads at the Kizhi Museum Complex
862. Flowers. Zhostovo tray. Artist B. Grafov
863. Churila Plenkovich. Palekh casket. 1934. Artist P. Bazhenov
865. Lacemaking

867

868

The acceptance of Christianity in 988 marked the start of a new historical period, linking Russia to Christian culture and making Christianity the basis of the way of life of its people. As Patriarch Alexis II of Moscow and All Russia said, the Russian Orthodox Church is a "unique custodian of the historical and cultural memory of our people ... Along with holy biblical memories, the church calendar ... cultivates the memory of the battles of Kulikovo, Poltava and Borodino." All main events in Russian history are closely associated with Orthodoxy. The popular belief in a single, holy, congregational, apostolic church helped the nation to overcome foreign invaders, defend its political independence and remain an Orthodox country. The path trodden by Russian Orthodox pastors and believers in the twentieth century was not an easy one. Orthodoxy was affected by all the tragic events — revolution, war and political repressions.

869

870

871

872

873

The faith of the elders in the Russian people, however, remained unshakeable. The level of faith of the Russian people was reflected in the extensive celebrations marking such memorial dates as the thousandth anniversary of the baptism of Russia in 1988 and the two-thousandth anniversary of Christianity in 2000.

Church life is experiencing a popular revival in the Russian Federation. Old churches are being restored, while new places of worship are built. Icons and other holy objects are being restored to their rightful places. Monasteries and seminaries are opening. The name of the Lord is worshipped in every corner of this vast country. The fifth among its sister churches, the Russian Church is a leading bastion of ecumenical Orthodoxy. Russia is a multi-confessional country, also inhabited by Muslims, Catholics, Buddhists, Jews and representatives of other religions.

874

875

876

877

878

867. Religious procession in memory of St Seraphim of Sarov in Nizhny Novgorod Region

868. Christ the Pantocrator. Mosaic. Church on the Spilled Blood in St Petersburg

869. Patriarch Alexis II

870. Konevets icon of the Mother of God in the Monastery on Konevets Island

871. Icon of the Smolensk Mother of God in the Church of Christ the Saviour in Moscow

872, 873, 876. Worshippers in the Intercession Cathedral in Krasnoyarsk

874, 877. In the Pskov Caves Dormition Monastery

875. Interior decor of the Transfiguration Church in Kizhi

878. Ceremonial procession with the Tikhvin icon of the Mother of God in the Pskov Caves Dormition Monastery, Pechory

Along with Orthodoxy and Protestantism, Roman Catholicism is one of the main Christian movements. Catholic churches were first built in Russia in the eighteenth century, during the reign of Catherine the Great. Political relations were established between Russia and Rome. The dialogue between the Vatican and Russia was revived in 1990, when diplomatic relations were restored with the Holy See. Catholic communities now exist in many towns of the Russian Federation.

879. Muslim women
880. Azimov Mosque in Kazan. 1890
881. St Petersburg Mosque's cupola
882. Start of the Muslim holy month of Ramadan
883. Manger outside the Church of the Immaculate Conception, Moscow
884, 885. Roman Catholic service
886, 888. Moscow Synagogue
887. St Petersburg Synagogue. 1883–93
889. Meditating monk in Sayan
890. Attribute of Buddhist ritual
891. Little monk
892. Interior of Kuntsechoinei Datsan in St Petersburg
893. Festival at a datsan in Buryatia

There are at least fifteen million adherents of Islam in Russia. They are mostly concentrated in the Volga region, Western Siberia, the Caucasus, Moscow Region. St Petersburg Mosque, when built, was the largest in Europe, and it is the most northern in the world. The main dogma of Islam is the belief that there is only one God but Allah and Mohammed is his messenger. Islam arose on the territory of the Russian Federation in 642, when Arabs came to what is now Daghestan. The practice of Islam is a vital element in the self-identification of the Tatar, Bashkir, Chechen, Daghestan and many other indigenous nations, reflecting their environments, education and the settings in which they grew up and live. A true Moslem does not limit himself to saying prayers or attending mosque. His aim is profound religious knowledge, mastering the wisdom of the Koran and following its tenets in everyday life. The Islamic peoples of the Russian Federation are currently experiencing a rise in religious self-consciousness and a ceremonial revival. The number of mosques is growing and new Islamic study centres are opening.

In 1841, Buddhism — in the form of Lamaism or Tibetan Buddhism — was recognised as one of the official religions of the Russian Empire. The first Buddhist university monastery — Tamchinsky Datsan — was founded in Buryatia. A datsan was even opened

in St Petersburg, the capital of the Russian Empire. Besides Buryatia, the other principal Buddhist region of Russia is Kalmykia. The capital of Kalmykia, Elista, is home to an Institute of the Rebirth of Buddhism.

Judaism is a traditional confession in Russia. Our country has the world's third largest number of Jewish religious communities after Israel and the United States. More than a hundred years ago, large synagogues were built in both Moscow and St Petersburg. Synagogues also function in many other towns.

895

896

897

898

899

The largest gas and oil producing country in the world lies between the Baltic Sea and the Pacific Ocean. Besides natural reserves of oil, gas and nickel, Russia also has an enormous industrial potential and highly trained scientific experts. As a result, Russian industry is world-famous for its high technological level and *science-intensive products*. The structure of the Russian industrial sector has not undergone any fundamental changes since the Soviet period. The correlations of the volumes of production in the different industries, however, have changed. Heavy machine construction is currently the leader

900
901
902

in this field, producing steam, gas and boiler equipment, gas turbine technologies, large motors and current isolators, steam turbines and boilers, steam generators and petroleum chemicals. Such produce successfully competes on both the domestic and foreign markets. The share of oil and gas mining, processing, metal working and fuel industry, electric energy, coloured and black metallurgy and food products in the total volume of Russian production has also risen. A major portion of budget resources has been allocated to their development. Although recent years have witnessed a growth in the rates of industrial production, Russian industry has clearly approached the maximum possible level of output under the existing technical capacity. It is now time to update the equipment, optimise the production processes, raise the degree of automation and retrain personnel.

←
894. Launching of Sputnik
895. Launching a Soyuz FG rocket with the Progress M-46 cargo ship at the Baikonur Cosmodrome
896. Niva-Chevrolet
897. Rocket plane design. Institute of Applied Mechanics, Russian Academy of Sciences
898. Painting the guns of a Russian warship
899. Apparatus for decontaminating water using ultraviolet rays invented by Novosibirsk scientists
900, 902, 904, 905. Mining and heavy industry form the basis of the Russian national economy
901. River Yenisei and Sayano-Shushenskaya Hydroelectric Dam
903. Third frigate launched at the Baltic Shipyard, St Petersburg
906. A Novosibirsk scientist has patented an invention reducing energy loss in electric apparatuses.

903
904
905

906

The armed forces exist to protect the territorial integrity of the State, not to attack other nations – such is Russia's military doctrine. This has always been a matter of principle in Russian military policy which has retained a defensive stance throughout history. Russia's armed forces comprise the Strategic Rocket Forces, the Air Force, the Ground Forces and the Navy. In line with the nation's Constitution, the President of the Russian Federation is the Supreme Commander-in-Chief of the armed forces.

The Russian Navy is made up of the Caspian Flotilla and the Baltic, Black Sea, Northern and Pacific Fleets. Russia's naval

907

908

909

Russia's army is the flesh of the flesh of the Russian people. Its mission is an arduous one, involving great risk and danger, though it is a noble mission too. An important role in ensuring Russia's national security as a major world power is played by the Rocket Forces, which form the country's nuclear shield. Their weapons include nuclear warheads mounted on intercontinental ballistic rockets. The S-300 anti-aircraft rocket systems can take down any craft of a probable aggressor, including the F-117

Stealth Fighter, the Tomahawk and unpiloted planes. Russia has also made unique discoveries that are as yet unattainable to other nuclear States. In September 2005 the Northern Fleet saw tests of the new Bulava intercontinental sea-based ballistic missile. The system can carry no fewer than ten individual nuclear units, and its range covers almost eight thousand kilometres.

Russian planes can carry out military operations anywhere from six hundred to one thousand five hundred kilometres from

910

911

912

913

914

base aerodromes. Russia's TU-160, also known as "Blackjack" is recognised as the world's most powerful bomber, while the SU-27 Front Line Fighter is considered the king of the skies. The multipurpose S-37 Berkut fighter leaves America's corresponding F-22A Raptor far behind in every respect. The Paratrooper Forces are used for special operations as well as peacekeeping tasks. They have proved themselves to be the best trained and most professional forces in the fight against terrorism and separatism.

Having a large Ground Force is of vital importance for Russia, which has very extensive land borders. The T-72 tank series is in use to this day in many countries throughout the world, while the T-90 was justly recognised as the finest model of the last century. Russia's next-generation BMP-3 infantry combat vehicle serves to assist tanks during battle as well as for transporting troops.

915

916

917

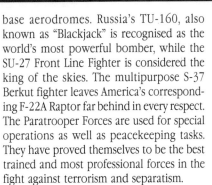

918

919

920

power is largely centred in the latter two. Rocket and nuclear submarines form the basis of the fighting efficiency of the Russian Navy, which also has the Admiral Kuznetsov *aircraft carrier at its disposal.*

907. Berkut (Golden Eagle) – multipurpose 5th generation fighter C-37
908, 909, 915, 918, 919. Daily life
910. Geiran landing craft and assaut boat
911. Topol mobile missile system
912. Buk-M1 unmanned anti-aircraft system
913. Peter the Great heavy nuclear missile cruiser
914. Multirole all-weather combat K-52 Alligator helicopter
916. Nuclear submarine delivering humanitarian cargo to Yamal Peninsula
917. Russian Army emblem
920. Gun-missile tank T-80

921

922

The cultural potential of the various people inhabiting the Russian Federation was formed over many centuries. The traditional heroic epics, chronicles, annals, birch-bark documents, church frescoes and Old Russian music reflect the high level of culture of all classes of people before the reforms of Peter the Great. The rapid development of education, art and science, which began in the late seventeenth century, transformed Russia into one of the leading world powers. The golden age of Russian culture was the nineteenth century, which gave the world the writings of Alexander Pushkin, Nikolai Gogol, Leo Tolstoy, Fedor Dostoyevsky and Anton Chekhov. The music of such famous composers as Modest Mussorgsky, Peter Tchaikovsky and Nikolai Rimsky-Korsakov rank among the finest achievements of world culture. In the early twentieth century, a movement known as the Russian avant-garde arose in the national school of painting. Singer Fedor Chaliapin and ballerinas Anna Pavlova and Tamara Karsavina shone

Post-war Russian literature has seen such figures as Alexander Tvardovsky, Alexander Solzhenitsyn, Valentin Rasputin, Yuri Trifonov, Vladimir Vysotsky, Iosif Brodsky and Bulat Okudzhava. Theatres staged plays by Viktor Rozov, Alexander Arbuzov, Alexander Volodin and Alexander Vampilov.

Leningrad's Bolshoi Drama Theatre and the Sovremennik, the Theatre on Malaya Bronnaya, the Taganka Theatre and the Lenin Komsomol Theatre in Moscow were all immensely popular. Cinemas screened films by Mikhail Romm, Marlen Khutsiev and Andrei Tarkovsky. Russian musicians, singers and ballet dancers earned international glory. Traditions born in the distant past continue to develop in Russian culture today.

923

924

925

926

927

on the stages of the imperial theatres. Russian opera and ballet stars performed in Sergei Diaghilev's *Saisons Russes*, causing a furore in Europe and revolutionising world theatre. The most important writers of the 1920s and 1930s were novelists Mikhail Sholokhov and Andrei Platonov and poets Sergei Yesenin, Vladimir Mayakovsky, Boris Pasternak and Osip Mandelstam. Composers Dmitry Shostakovich and Sergei Prokofiev wrote music, while Russian ballet stars danced in the world's top theatres. Konstantin Stanislavsky, Vladimir Nemirovich-Danchenko and Vsevolod Meyerhold staged famous plays. The films of Sergei Eisenstein, Vsyevolod Pudovkin and Olexandr Dovzhenko are now regarded as masterpieces of world cinema.

921. Diana Vishneva and Andrian Fadeev in Balanchine's *Jewels*
922. Cheburashka — popular hero of children's cartoons and official mascot of the Russian XX Winter Olympics Squad in Turin
923. Conductor Valery Gergiev
924. Mstislav Rostropovich conducting
925. Coductor Gennadi Rozhdestvensky
926. Violinist Vadim Repin
927. Performance of Giuseppe Verdi's opera *Rigoletto* at the Galina Vishnevskaya Centre of Opera Singing
928. Contestants at the XII Peter Tchaikovsky International Competition of Vocalists in Moscow
929. Pianist Nikolai Petrov
930. Premiere of concert performance of Dmitry Shostakovich's opera *Lady Macbeth of Mtsensk District* at the Moscow Conservatoire
931. Conductor Yury Temirkanov
932. Writer Alexander Solzhenitsyn
933. Singer Elena Obraztsova
934. Singer Dmitry Hvorostovsky
935. Film director Andrei Konchalovsky
936. Film director Nikita Mikhalkov
937. Mikhail Piotrovsky, director of the State Hermitage Museum, in his office
938. Scene from Modest Mussorgsky's opera *Boris Godunov* at the opening of the 225th season at the Bolshoi Theatre
939. Performance of Anton Chekhov's play *Uncle Vanya* at the Golden Mask Festival

940 941

942

The popular notion of Russia as a land of endless winters, bears roaming the streets and bearded peasants downing shots of vodka and playing the balalaika is now firmly in the past. Russia has discarded its bast shoes and successfully assimilated all civilised forms of life.

In the majority of towns and cities across the country, guests from Europe and overseas encounter everything to which they are accustomed at home — hotels, restaurants, night clubs, bars, discos, casinos, billiard rooms, bowling alleys, car parks, saunas and swimming pools — with all levels of service, including VIP.

The most active and refined social spots in Russia are to be found in Moscow, with St Petersburg far behind in second place. Equipped with the latest electronic and digital technologies, groundbreaking designs and glamorous and professional personnel, the Moscow hospitality and leisure industry corresponds to the highest world standards.

943 944

946

945

947

Ten years ago, there were only a few Western-style restaurants in Russia. Russian establishments have now achieved such mastery that they can successfully complete with many European professionals.

The restaurant business develops in Russia in three main directions — fast food, medium price range and haute cuisine. Not only have fast food chains become respectable, they have gone multinational.

940. Il Patio Daria restaurant
     on October Field in Moscow
941. Moscow by night
942. Break dancing competition
943, 944. Show of the Vyacheslav
     Zaitsev collection
945. Opening at the Russian Academy
     of Arts
946. White Night in St Petersburg
947. New Year in a children's
     department store in Moscow
948. City advertisement in night-time
     Moscow
949. Moscow. Arbat Square
950. To the sound of jazz
951. Pop concert
952. *Dancing for Survival* show
     at the Reverie Night Club
     in Moscow
953. Roulette
954. Playoffs for the world
     championships and the Russia
     Cup at the Megasphere Bowling
     Club in Moscow
955. Competition of hair stylists
956. New Arbat by night
957. Disco

Many famous world brands now have their own clothes, accessory and jewellery outlets in Moscow, St Petersburg and other Russian cities. This does not abrogate the concept of "Russian vogue," which is more than capable of competing on the international level. Russian seasonal *prêt-à-porter* evokes the constant interest of Western buyers and journalists. Several Russian fashion houses and design studios are known throughout the world. The Russian beauty industry is equally successful. The national hairdressing team has performed so well in international competitions that the World Congress of Hairdressers in Las Vegas decided to hold the XXI World Championship for Hairdressing, Decorative Cosmetics and Nail Design in Moscow in 2006.

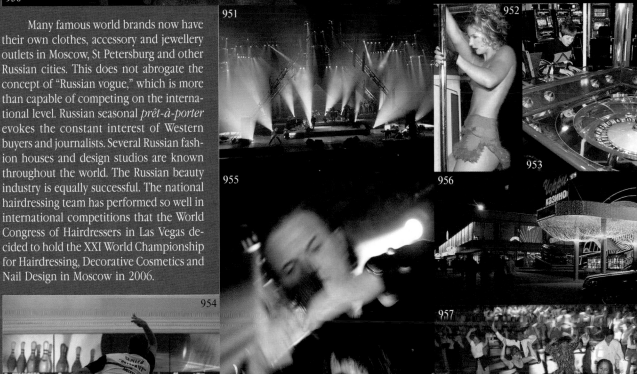

R U S S I A

TEXTS
Boris Antonov, Lydia Liakhovskaya, Yury Mudrov, Pavel Pavlinov, Nathalia Popova, Galina Vasilieva-Shliapina

TRANSLATION FROM THE RUSSIAN BY Kenneth MacInnes, Valery Fateev, Gillian Kenyon, Julia Redkina

DESIGN Denis Lazarev

PHOTOGRAPHS
Viacheslav Alferov, Alexei Babaev, Valentin Baranovsky, Valery Barnev, Nikolai Berketov, Leonid Bogdanov, Serguei Chistobaev, Vladimir Davydov, Pavel Demidov, Vladimir Denissov, Vladimir Dorokhov, Anatoly Falamov, Andrei Fefelov, Vladimir Filippov, Alexander Fomitchev, Valery Gordt, Valery Goretsky, Oleg Grigorov, Yury Grigorov, Leonid Guerkus, Pavel Ivanov, Alexander Kashnitsky, Leonard Kheifets, Vladimir Khmelevsky, Artur Kirakozov, Adam Kirilenko, Konstantin Kokoshkin, Victor Kornushin, Alexei Korotaev, Serguei Kozlov, Evgueny Kretchmar, Serguei Kristev, Denis Lazarev, Lydia Liakhovskaya, Mikhail Manin, Pavel Mayorov, Vladimir Melnikov, Yury Molodkovets, Yury Morozov, Andrei Nikolaev, Nathalia Onichtenko, Alexander Petrosian, Andrei Petrosian, Marina Petrovskaya, Dmitry Petrovsky, Serguei Podmetin, Victor Poliakov, Nikolai Rakhmanov, Victor Savik, Georgy Shablovsky, Alexander Shpikalov, Evgueny Siniaver, Victor Solomatin, Vladimir Stoliarov, Vladimir Terebenin, Oleg Trubsky, Alexei Vasiliev, Vladimir Vdovin, Alexander Viktorov, Serguei Voronin, Vasily Vorontsov, Kira Zharinova

EDITORS
Irina Lvova, Irina Kharitonova

SELECTION OF ILLUSTRATIONS Anna Barshai, Elena Demidova, Ninel Yakovleva

ENGLISH TEXT EDITOR Elena Shabalova

COMPUTER LAYOUT Nina Sokolova

COLOUR CORRECTION
Vladimir Kniazev, Alexander Kondratov, Tatiana Krakovskaya, Alexander Miagkov

SEPARATION AND IMPOSITION
Viacheslav Bykovski, Dmitry Chubarov, Dmitry Trofimov

P-2 Art Publishers, 11 Zvenigorodskaya St, Saint Petersburg, 191119 Russia. Fax/Tel.: +7 (812) 320 92 01